Strategy Formulation: Political Concepts

The West Series in Business Policy and Planning

Consulting Editors
Charles W. Hofer
Dan Schendel

Strategy Formulation: Analytical Concepts
Charles W. Hofer and Dan Schendel

Strategy Implementation: The Role of Structure and Process
Jay R. Galbraith and Daniel A. Nathanson

Organizational Goal Structures
Max D. Richards

Strategy Formulation: Political Concepts
Ian C. MacMillan

Strategy Formulation: Political Concepts

Ian C. MacMillan
Columbia University

West Publishing Company
St. Paul   New York   Los Angeles   San Francisco

Library of Congress Cataloging in Publication Data

MacMillan, Ian, 1940–
      Strategy formulation.
      (The West series in business policy and planning)
      Bibliography: p.
      Includes index.
      1. Corporate planning. 2. Organizational behavior. 3. Interorganizational relations.

I. Title.
HD30.28.M28   658.4'01   78–1848
ISBN 0-8299-0209-0

To Georg Marais who got me started.
To my wife Jean who kept me going.

*

Contents

*

Foreword

The purpose of this common foreword to all the volumes in the *West Series on Business Policy and Planning* is threefold: first, to provide background to the reader on the origins and purposes of the series; second, to describe the overall design of the series and the contents of the texts contained in the series; and third, to describe ways in which the series or the individual texts within it can be used.

This series is a response to the rapid and significant changes that have occurred in the policy area over the past fifteen years. While business policy is a subject of long standing in management schools, it has traditionally been viewed as a capstone course whose primary purpose was to *integrate* the knowledge and skills students had gained in the functional disciplines. During the past decade, however, policy has developed a substantive content of its own that has permitted it to emerge as a discipline in its own right. Originally, this content focused on the concept of organizational strategy and on the processes by which such strategies were formulated and implemented within organizations. More recently, the scope of the field has broadened to include the study of all the functions and responsibilities of top management, together with the organizational processes and systems for formulating and implementing organizational strategy. To date, however, this extension in scope has not been reflected in texts in the field.

The basic purpose of the *West Series on Business Policy and Planning* is to fill this void through the development of a series of texts that cover the policy field while incorporating the latest research findings and conceptual thought.

In designing the series, we took care to ensure, not only that the various texts fit together as a series, but also that each text is self-contained and addresses a major topic in the field. In addition, each text is written so that it can be used at both the advanced undergraduate and the masters level. The first four texts, which cover topics in the heart of the policy field, are:

Organizational Goal Structures, by Max D. Richards.

Strategy Formulation: Analytical Concepts, by Charles W. Hofer and Dan Schendel.

Strategy Formulation: Political Concepts, by Ian C. MacMillan.

Strategy Implementation: The Role of Structure and Process, by Jay R. Galbraith and Daniel A. Nathanson.

A second set of texts are in preparation and should be available next year. They will cover additional topics in policy and planning such as the behavioral and social systems aspects of the strategy formulation process, environment forecasting, strategic control, formal planning systems, and the strategic management of new ventures. Additional texts covering still other topics are being considered for the years following.

The entire series has been designed so that the texts within it can be used in several ways. First, the individual texts can be used to supplement the conceptual materials contained in existing texts and case books in the field. In this regard, explicit definitions are given for those terms and concepts for which there is as yet no common usage in the field, and, whenever feasible, the differences between these definitions and those in the major texts and case books are noted. Second, one or more of the series texts can be combined with cases drawn from the Intercollegiate Case Clearing House to create a hand-crafted case course suited to local needs. To assist those interested in such usage, most texts in the series include a list of ICCH cases that could be used in conjunction with it. Finally, the series can be used without other materials by those who wish to teach a theory-oriented policy course. Thus, the series offers the individual instructor flexibility in designing a policy course. Finally, because of their self-contained nature, each of the texts can also be used as a supplement to various nonpolicy courses within business and management school curricula.

Charles W. Hofer

Dan Schendel

Consulting Editors

September, 1977

Preface

This textbook is intended for both practicing managers and business management students. It provides a framework for thinking about strategy with an interorganizational perspective. The thrust of the argument is that managers, as strategists, must take into account the behavioral and political components of human action when they formulate the strategies that will ensure the success of the organizations they manage.

The text is structured in such a way that the initial chapters are rich in concept. This conceptual material is systematically developed into a practical framework for political strategy formulation, so that, by the end of the book, the whole focus is on practical application. In the last part of the text, three case studies are analyzed thoroughly to show the applicability of the theory.

To avoid cumbersome references within the text, the source material on which the reasoning was based is listed in a bibliography at the end of the text. Those interested in pursuing specific topics in more depth should refer to the works listed. These works have been held to a minimum.

The intent of the textbook is to provide a broad delineation of the field of political strategy. The reader should emerge in the end with some systematic concepts about formulating political strategy. These should complement the approaches to strategy formulation that have been discussed in the other books in the *West Series on Business Policy and Planning*.

1

The Political Perspective

THE PURPOSE OF THIS TEXT

This textbook is designed to help students and practitioners of business policy develop an understanding of the political component of business behavior and organizational strategy. Because the perspective of this text is political, it is possible to apply the concepts in the text to contexts outside of business. The principles that will be discussed have been applied to hospitals, church groups, nonprofit organizations, and other organizations.

The book is intended to complement the writings of the other authors in *the West Series on Business Policy*, and it tries assiduously to avoid repetition of the work on business strategies by Hofer and Schendel, on organizational goal by Richards, and on strategy implementation by Galbraith and Nathanson.

The focus of this text is on politics, intraorganizational and interorganizational, and it tries to develop pragmatic and useful models for use by the general managers in their efforts to balance the demands being pressed on them by disparate, and perhaps powerful, interest groups inside and outside their organizations.

AN OUTLINE OF THIS TEXT

The direction of the argument in this text can be followed by referring to Figure 1.1, which is a much simplified outline of the material to be discussed in this textbook.   As a result of the environmental analysis (discussed by Hofer and Schendel), the organization perceives certain *threats and opportunities*.   The first step in the political approach is to carry out a systems analysis in order that determines who the *key actors* are who influence these threats and opportunities.   Other organizations that will benefit from the opportunities can be identified, and these organizations become potential allies of the organization that seeks to take advantage of the opportunity.   On the other hand, other organizations that pose the threats are potential opponents of the organization.

The political strategy formulation approach recognizes that, where it is legal, the firm will seek out these allies to help achieve its goals. At the beginning of this political strategy approach, it is necessary to determine the relative *power and influence* of the firm.   On the basis of its power and influence, the firm can find a sense of what it can accomplish without forming an alliance.   With this knowledge, the firm can determine its *negotiating base*—the minimum it will be prepared to accept when it forges an negotiated alliance with its allies. The negotiating base provides the foundation for a negotiating strategy by which the firm can go out and form an alliance with those organizations that can assist it in achieving its goals.

The firm, therefore, *selects potential allies* and then carries out a detailed internal and external *political systems analysis* of its allies in order to determine what *their* power and influence are and what strengths and weaknesses *they* have.   The firm then carries out *negotiations* that result in the formation of an alliance.   If this is successful, the alliance can turn attention to their potential opponents.

As before, the internal and external *political systems of the opponents* are analyzed in order to develop an idea of what the *opponents'* power and influence are and where *their* strengths and weaknesses lie. This analysis provides the basis for the formulation of *offensive strategies* aimed at taking advantage of those opportunities in which the alliance can use its strengths and *defensive strategies* aimed at avoiding or countering weaknesses that reinforce the threats facing the alliance.   As these strategies are identified, the alliance can anticipate what *counterresponses* can be expected from the opponents. Some strategies can be countered easily; others can be more difficult for the opponents to counter.   Thus, a best set of offensive and de-

Figure 1.1. Schematic Outline of Political Strategy Formulation.

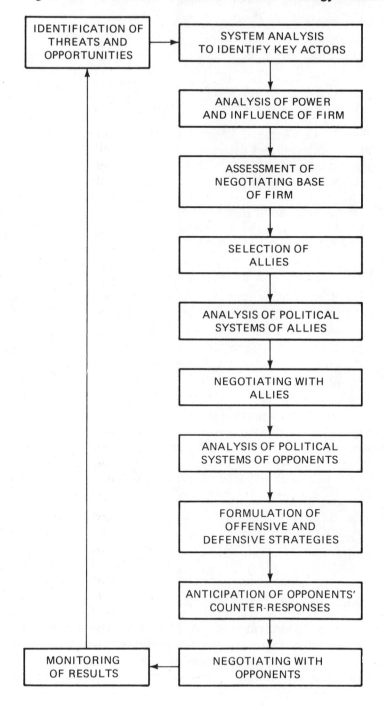

fensive strategies can be determined, and the strategic counter-responses of opponents to these strategies determined.

The alliance then launches its offensive and defensive strategies. After they have been launched, it is often necessary to come to an agreement with the opponents in order to avoid mutually destructive conflict. Hence, a negotiating strategy must be formulated to prepare for these critical *negotiations with opponents*.

After the strategies have been launched, the progress of these strategies is *monitored*, and the results then are used to reinitiate the environmental analysis. Thus, the identification of new threats and opportunities is achieved.

It can be seen that this approach requires the investigation of many phenomena that are not handled in traditional textbooks on strategy. We need to pay attention to such topics as power, influence, negotiation, political analysis, and anticipation of strategic countermoves, among others. In this text, these topics will be explored systematically, starting with very basic and fundamental concepts and developing into fairly elaborate models with a deliberately political perspective.

In chapter 2, the concept of manipulation is explained. We try to unfold what such phenomena as power, influence, and authority really mean, and, given these insights, we try to explain what the bases of power, influence, and authority are. How does one become influential? What contributes to power? With the answers to these questions, it is possible to formulate guidelines for developing power and influence that can be used to structure the behavior of opponents so that the organization can achieve its ends.

In chapter 3, the discussion focuses upon negotiation. In particular, we look at what is called *distributive bargaining*, which is akin to negotiating with an opponent about "how big a piece of a pie" the organization and its opponent will get. Tactics for handling such situations are developed, and the tactics of bluffing, threatening, and promising are analyzed in detail. Then, attention is given to the development of a negotiating strategy, which focuses on the entire negotiation process and integrates the various bluffs, threats, and promises that are required to handle each issue that arises in a complex negotiation.

Chapter 4 takes a deliberately political perspective and examines the behavior of an individual within a complex organization. From this political model of individual behavior is traced the formation of coalitions and interest groups in organizations.

In chapter 5, the whole process of policy formulation and execution in a political structure within the organization is developed. The importance of this model for political strategy—in the process of manipulating and/or accommodating the environment in order to achieve corporate goals—is discussed.

Chapter 6 highlights interorganizational relations. The various political moves that an organization can take under different environmental structures are identified. At the end of the section, guidelines for developing a political thrust in different environments are suggested. Then, attention is given to the problem of strategic anticipation: what responses can opponents make to an organization's strategies, and which responses are they likely to make? Several guidelines for strategic anticipation are provided.

Chapter 7 turns to the concept of political strategy formulation— the formulation of a manipulative and/or accommodative strategy that will so structure conditions in the organization's environment that the corporate strategy is achieved. A broad set of guidelines is developed that elaborates upon the outline given in Figure 1.1.

In chapters 8, 9, and 10, three cases are discussed. Specific facets of the political strategy formulation process are highlighted in the analysis of these cases, which are used to illustrate the application of many of the principles explained in this text.

A NOTE ON ETHICS

It should be noted that there is a danger that these concepts can be used unethically. While I am concerned with bad ethics, I can prescribe no specific ethical stance. It is not for me to dictate ethics to the reader. My purpose is to explore phenomena that have been observed in practice but have been underemphasized in theory until now. I draw many disguised examples from practice in order to illustrate the concepts. These examples are neither condoned nor condemned; they are all real-life examples observed in practice and reported as such.

Each reader has his own set of ethics,[1] but, in reading this book, he should recognize three things.

1. The concepts discussed in this text can be used without overstepping any personal ethical limits.

[1] Throughout this text, except in actual case examples, the terms *he* and *his* will be used as referents for *person* without regard to the actual sex of the individual involved.

2.   The concepts may alert the reader to alternatives that less ethical opponents might use.

3.   The book is international in scope, and we should keep in mind that there are many ethical systems in the world's nations.

2

Power, Influence, and Organizational Politics

WHAT IS ORGANIZATIONAL POLITICS?

- In October 1976, *Fortune* reported that the chief executive of a large building materials company, which had been in the doldrums, had succeeded in reawakening the company and had transformed it to such an extent that in five years net profits had risen 115 percent. However, as a result of a series of maneuvers by a group of outside directors, he was replaced overnight, to the astonishment of everyone but the directors.

- The general manager of a regional soap company was about to announce his decision to take over a smaller food company when several senior managers threatened to resign en bloc if the funds were not deployed instead to expanding the soap operation. His reliance on their rare skills in soap making forced him to postpone the acquisition.

- A small manufacturer of truck seats developed a new, more comfortable, back-supporting seat that he was having trouble marketing to truck manufacturers. He convinced the truckers' union to demand these seats and have their demands written into their contract.

When we think about each one of these incidents, it becomes clear that not one of them could have occurred without some kind of political activity. In each case, there are similarities, as well as differences.

Let us explain similarities first. In each case, there was some kind of conflict in goals between actors. The term *actor* is used generically to mean a person, a group, an organization, or even a nation. In each case, one actor achieved its goal by carrying out an action that distracted the other actor from achieving its goal. This suggests a basic concept that can be used to develop a definition of political action: "Political action takes place when an actor, recognizing that the achievement of its goal is influenced by the behavior of other actors in the situation, undertakes action against the others to ensure that its own goals are achieved."

This working definition of political action will be used throughout this book. There must be at least two people in order for political action to take place. If the first person recognizes that the attainment of his goals is going to be influenced by the behavior of the other and undertakes some action against that other to ensure that his goal is achieved, that action can be construed as political for the purposes of this book.

Let us now explore the differences in the examples at the beginning of the chapter. In the first place, there is a difference of *level* of action. The seat manufacturer was clearly operating at an *interorganizational* level. He went out to another organization in the environment and restructured the situation, so that his goal (of selling seats and making profits) was enhanced. Clearly, the soap manufacturer was operating at an *intraorganizational* level. The conflict was contained within the ranks of the organization itself. In the case of the building materials company, we see a gray area, where it is not clear whether we are looking at action inside the organization (board level) or outside the organization (outside directors). However, these examples do help illustrate that politics can take place at various levels in the organization—a topic to be explored more fully in later chapters.

The second major difference in the examples emerges when we look at the *direction* employed. The soap manufacturer bowed to the *direct* threats of the key subordinates who initiated the action. The truck manufacturers acceded to the demands of the truckers' union; yet the action was not initiated by them but by the seat manufacturer. Clearly, there are two major alternatives in political action: *direct* action and *indirect* action. These, too, will be explored later.

The third major difference in the examples lies in the *way* in which the actors went about achieving their purposes. The board of directors had the *authority* to replace the chief executive. The soap manufacturer's subordinates resorted to *threats,* because they lacked the authority to overrule their superior. The seat manufacturer resorted to *persuading* the trucking union to support him and the union then *negotiated* an agreement with the truck manufacturers.

One gets a sense that in the different cases we are seeing the outcome of such phenomena as power, influence, and authority within organizations or between organizations. Often, terms such as "power" and "influence" are used generically or synonymously in everyday language. In the next section, these concepts will be explored in more detail, so that, for the purposes of this discussion, we have a clear idea of what is meant by power and influence.

The reasoning in these next sections comes mainly from the work of Blau (1969), Thompson (1967), Parsons (1969), Chamberlain (1955), and Pettigrew (1973).

MANIPULATIVE ACTIVITY

This section discusses the concept of *manipulation*; that is, the activity under taken *unilaterally* by an actor in order to get an opponent to behave as the actor wishes. This is in contrast to accommodative action, in which the actor undertakes action with the intent of coming to *joint agreement* as to how the actor *and* the opponents will behave.

Thus, manipulation is a process whereby a manipulator unilaterally restructures conditions in the environment in such a way that the opponents decide on courses of action desirable to the manupulator. How can the manipulator accomplish this? He must somehow find a way of getting the opponents to act as he wishes—they must *decide* to act in ways that suit the manipulator, rather than in other ways. It is in intervening in the opponents' decision-making process that the key to manipulation lies.

In deciding on a course of action, the opponents must assess the effects of alternate courses of action on their aspirations. Each person has some structure of aspirations against which he compares the alternatives. The opponent will judge the positive and negative connotations of each of the alternatives being considered and, on a highly personal basis, develop some measure of satisfaction with the outcomes of the alternatives. The alternative with the highest level of satisfaction then will be selected.

Figure 2.1. Simple Example.

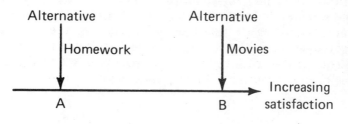

- A very simple two-alternative situation is illustrated in Figure 2.1. Suppose a child must choose between doing homework and going to the movies. Both alternatives have both positive and negative connotations for him. Doing homework means that he gets approval from parents and teachers and increases his chances of getting a high grade. However, he may find it boring and tiresome. Going to the movies promises to be enjoyable and exciting. However, it costs part of his allowance and leaves him with feelings of guilt afterwards. In the absence of intervention by a manipulator, he will weigh the alternatives in terms of his assessment of the positive and negative connotations of both alternatives. Let us suppose that the balance of these results in measures of satisfaction that lie at A and B on his scale of increasing satisfaction in Figure 2.1. B clearly lies at a higher level of satisfaction than A, so he will elect to go to the movies. If his parents are to manipulate this situation, they must intervene in this process and cause him to select actions that suit them. Such manipulation will be explored next.

MEANS OF MANIPULATION

Here, we identify the *means* by which an individual can manipulate a situation. The reasoning closely parallels that of Parsons (1969) who identifies two channels of manipulation and two modes of manipulation.

CHANNELS OF MANIPULATION

The opponent makes decisions on the basis of his *perception* of the environment surrounding him. Thus, we can conceive of two possible *channels* for getting the opponent to rerank the alternatives and select the alternative the manipulator desires.

Situational Channel

First, the manipulator can change the structure of the *situation* in which the opponent is placed. In the light of this changed situation, the opponent may decide on a course of action that he would otherwise not have chosen. In other words, by rearrangements of things or people in the *situation itself*, the structure of the situation is changed, and this results in manipulated action. (Examples will be given later.)

Intentional Channel

Alternatively, the manipulator can attempt to change the opponent's *intentions*, not by restructuring the situation but by communicating with the opponent in such a way that the opponent's perceptions of the situation change. In the light of his changed perception of the situation, the opponent may change his intentions and decide on a new course of action that he otherwise would not have chosen.[1]

The manipulator has another dimension by which to structure these decision alternatives, namely, by the use of positive and negative modes of action.

Figure 2.2.   Positive Mode of Manipulation.

Figure 2.2(a) *Original situation*

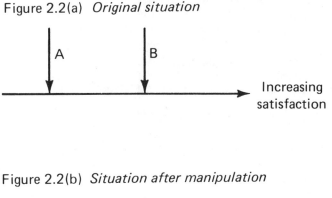

Figure 2.2(b) *Situation after manipulation*

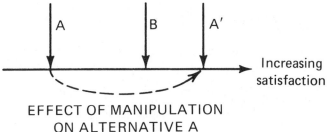

EFFECT OF MANIPULATION
ON ALTERNATIVE A

MODES OF MANIPULATION

If the manipulator uses the positive mode, then the opponent feels better off as a result of the manipulation. If the manipulator uses

---

[1] While the two channels identified here are the same at the psychological level, this method of differentiating between types of action proves useful at the political level.

a negative mode, then the opponent feels worse off. These situations are illustrated in Figures 2.2 and 2.3.

In Figure 2.2, the positive mode is illustrated. In the first part of the figure, the original situation is depicted. Clearly, the opponent would choose alternative action B over action A. However, the manipulator would prefer that action A be selected. In the second part of Figure 2.2, the situation after the manipulator has intervened by using the positive mode is shown. In some way or another, the alternative A has been moved to A', and the opponent will select A' and *at the same time feel better off*, because the level of satisfaction of choosing the desired action A' is higher than the original level of satisfaction of the original best alternative B.

The negative mode of manipulation is shown in Figure 2.3. In the first part, the opponent would choose action B, rather than action A. However, the manipulator would prefer him to choose action A. In the second part of the figure, the position after the manipulator has acted in a negative mode is depicted.

Figure 2.3. Negative Mode of Manipulation.

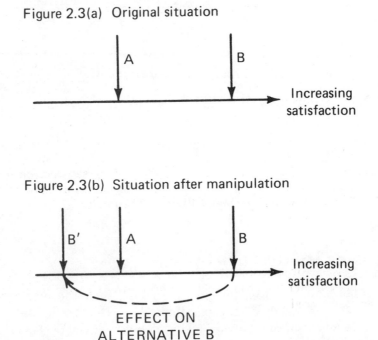

Figure 2.3(a) Original situation

Figure 2.3(b) Situation after manipulation

The manipulator has caused the satisfaction associated with action B to move down to B', and the opponent will select action A but will feel worse off, since the outcome is less satisfactory to him than before the manipulative action.

Having identified two channels and two modes of manipulative action it is now possible to combine these dimensions and identify and label four major means of manipulation.

FOUR MEANS OF MANIPULATION

The two dimensions combined produce four general ways of manipulating an opponent.   (See Figure 2.4.)

Figure 2.4. Four Means of Manipulation.

		Channel	
		Situational	Intentional
Mode	Positive	Inducement	Persuasion
	Negative	Coercion	Obligation

Inducement

The manipulator attempts to change the *structure of the situation,* so that the opponent's circumstances are *improved* by the selection of the alternative desired.

- For instance, suppose a manager wanted to quit his job to join another organization. The boss could offer him a large salary increase to make him stay. If the manager decides to stay, he will have been induced by the offer of extra salary and will feel better off as a result of doing so. His feelings toward the manipulation will be *positive.*

Coercion

The manipulator attempts to *change the situation's* structure, so that the opponent's circumstances are *aggravated* by not selecting the alternative desired.

- For instance, suppose the manager wanted to quit and the boss threatened to get court injunctions preventing him from leaving because of an employment contract he signed, or suppose that the manager threatened to blacklist him in the industry. The manager might decide to stay but

would feel worse off as a result.   His feelings towards the manipulation
would be *negative*.

Persuasion

The manipulator does not attempt to change the situation but pre-
sents arguments and logic to the opponent, showing that acting as
the manipulator desires corresponds better with the opponent's
achievement of satisfaction than the opponent originally perceived.
If the manipulator is successful, the opponent will commit himself
to the desired alternative and feel that he has gained by doing so.

- For instance, if the manager in the previous examples announced his intention to quit and the boss started to argue that the real challenge for
  managers lies in the present organization and that anyone staying with
  the organization would be virtually guaranteed a successful future, and
  so on, he might be able to persuade the manager that, in fact, it is better to stay with the present organization.   If this persuasive argument
  were successful, the manager would feel that he has benefited by the decision to stay and would feel positive about the manipulation.

Obligation

The manipulator directs to the opponent logic or argument that
shows that the opponent's original perception of the alternatives was
not correct and that, in fact, the alternative the opponent was considering selecting was not in keeping with the values the opponent
holds.   If the attempt is successful, the opponent selects the alternative the manipulator desires but feels worse off as a result.   However, as much as the opponent might wish to select the original alternative, he feels obligated to select the desired alternative.

- For instance, the boss of the manager might make him feel obligated to
  stay with his present organization because his present employers have
  invested a great deal of money and effort in training him in the skills
  for which he has been offered the new job.   He might feel obligated to
  stay but somewhat unhappy about doing so.

These four means of manipulation are presented in abstract, pure
form for discussion purposes only.   In practice, a manipulator might
try combinations of these means to effect the desired responses on
the part of the opponent.   However, these four means of manipulation do help clarify what is being attempted in a manipulation and,
in particular, allow for more precise definitions of power and influence than are obtained in everyday language.

POWER, INFLUENCE,
AND AUTHORITY

In this section, definitions of power, influence, and authority are developed, not because of a gratuitous desire to have a unique set of definitions, but because the next section uses these definitions for developing some operational ideas about the basis of power and how one might go about analyzing a situation in order to develop power in a situation.

DEFINITION OF POWER

Power of an actor *over an opponent* in a situation is the *capacity* of the actor to restructure the situation, so that the opponent acts as the actor wishes.

Power *in a situation* is regarded as the *capacity* of an actor (person, group, organization, nation) in that situation to manipulate via the *structural channel*. That is, power is the actor's capacity to restructure the *situation* in such a way as to get others to act as the actor desires.

There are several things worth noting about these definitions. First, power is *situationally* determined. That is, one's power is a a function of the situation, and power in one situation (at work) does not necessarily mean power in another situation (at home). Second, we need to distinguish between power *over specific actors* and power *in a situation*. The power one has in a situation is a function of the power one has over all the individual actors in that situation. Third, power is a *capacity*. One does not have to *use* power to *have* it. The recognition of the power *capacity* of an actor by its opponents affects the moves that they consider. The actor need not necessarily exercise that capacity in order to have an effect on the opponents' actions.

DEFINITION OF INFLUENCE

Influence of an actor *over an opponent* in a situation is the capacity of that actor to restructure the *perceptions* of the opponent so as to get the opponent to act as desired.

Influence of an actor *in a situation* is the capacity of the actor to restructure the *perception* of the opponents in the situation and get them to act as desired.

Obviously, in any real-life situation, an actor can use both power and influence, so we need a generic word to signify the sum of power and influence. For want of a catchall word, a new one will be coined.

DEFINITION OF POLITICAL CAPABILITY

Political capability is used to denote the sum of power and influence of an actor.

DEFINITION OF AUTHORITY

Authority is defined as *legitimized political capability;* that is, legitimized power and influence.

To the extent that an organization allows a person to induce, coerce, persuade, and obligate others, that person has legitimate power and influence and hence legitimate *formal* authority.

To the extent that people in the organization who are being induced, coerced, persuaded, and obligated by an individual feel that these actions are legitimate, the individual has legitimate power and influence and hence legitimate *informal* authority.

The *actual* authority of a person in a situation is really his informal authority in the situation. This informal authority can be greater or smaller than the formal authority conferred on the person by the organization.

Why then do we need to have formal authority in an organization? If there were not some kind of ballpark within which the members of an organization had to operate, the organization would become paralyzed by people trying to sort out the limits of their authority in the face of counteraction by others. The formal authority attached to various positions in an organization sets a datum from which individuals cannot move too far without serious resistance from other members of the firm. The larger the organization, the more important it is to have this datum.

Let us explore the concept of authority a little further.

• The very fact that you are reading this book means that some kind of authority has been conferred on me, even though we have never met. The major component of my authority is influence, rather than power. I am trying to change your perceptions of the world in which you live. To the extent that you have been required to read this book, I have formal authority. To the extent that I can persuade you in the opening chapters that the book is worth reading, I will start developing informal authority. If I asked you to turn now to page 100 and read it before continuing here, many of you probably would do it. You would feel I have a legitimate right to get you to do this. If, however, I asked you to go out and purchase a certain brand of toothpaste, very few of you would feel that I have a right to influence you in this way. I would have over-stepped the informal authority you grant me.

The point is that there are limits to authority, and these limits are broadly set by the organization in a formal sense, yet they are *specifically* set by each individual in the situation in an informal sense. The informal authority granted to a person in a situation is decided by each other person in the situation, and what may constitute a legitimate action by some may not be regarded as legitimate by others who may feel that the actor is overstepping the mark. One need only look to the protests against the Vietnam War for a very visible example of this phenomenon, during which the power and influence of the government were challenged by people who felt that the government was exceeding its legitimate authority.

At this point, it is appropriate to turn to the more pragmatic discussion of how these concepts are applied in political strategy formulation. What we are concerned with here is the question of what constitutes a basis for power and influence in a situation.

BASES OF POWER

The purpose of these two sections on the bases of power and influence is to unfold what appears to be the general characteristics of a situation that determine the political capability of an actor in a situation. This is done in the context of business organizations. Since power and influence are specific to a situation, it is very difficult to identify specific bases of power and influence—the source of political capability varies from situation to situation, and we would end up with an immense check list of little practical value. However, it is possible to identify, in general, what the source of power and influence in a situation is. From these general concepts, the source of power and influence in a specific situation can be identified by analyzing that situation.

The basis of power rests in the ability to restructure situations. The work of writers such as Blau (1969), Thompson, (1967), Emerson (1962), and Crozier (1971) suggests that there are several factors that contribute to power.

POSSESSION OF
STRATEGIC POWER RESOURCES

If one is to be in a position to restructure a situation, one needs the the resources to do so. So much is obvious. However, since power is situation specific, the resources required are situation specific, and it is pointless to try to list all the possible resources that could be important sources of power. Almost any resource could, in specific circumstances, be an important power resource.

It is useful to unfold the *characteristics* of the resource that makes it a power resource in a situation. Then, by analysis of a situation, one can determine which resources are or will be important determinants of the power base.

First it is important to recognize that a power resource must be *applicable* to the situation. Resources are deployed to induce or to coerce. If the resource cannot be used either to induce or to coerce or to resist an inducement or coercion from the opponent, then it is not valuable as a power base.

- For instance, all the very sophisticated, modern military equipment of advanced nations (such as supersonic fighters) is not appropriate to guerrilla warfare in dense jungles. In a situation such as that, a dedicated man or woman who is prepared to live under the most debilitating conditions could be a more important resource.

- Similarly, resources such as production capacity and stockpiles of raw materials are not useful to a firm that is in the throes of an industry recession, but they are in the case of a firm in the middle of an industry boom.

The last example allows us to introduce two other concepts that are important in assessing the value of resources as a power base, and these are *convertibility* and *timing*.

Production capacity is often far more difficult to convert into other resources (such as cash) than, say, raw material stockpiles. Thus, it is *convertibility*, coupled with *timing*, that determines the *strategic* nature of power resources.

- For instance, in many smaller economies, the building industry suffers chronic shortages; and the companies that are able to convert their resources in time to meet these shortages tend to prosper, those that cannot tend to founder. A typical pattern might be this. There is an undersupply of cement during a boom. Companies scramble to secure cement only to find that supply sources are committed to the more aggressive and far-thinking competitors. After losing a great deal of business and incurring heavy expenses securing cement supplies, the companies find that there is adequate cement but a shortage of skilled labor—they have the material but not the labor. Having gotten the labor, there is a shortage of funds to support working capital. In each case, it takes a great deal of effort to secure the strategic resources required at the time by converting existing resources that are not strategically valuable to resources that are.

Generally, a resource is strategic in a power context when there is an undersupply, or close to it, *and* when it is difficult or costly for the various competitors to convert existing resources into the strategic resource.

- Thus, crude oil *became* a strategic resource (and still is one) only after the OPEC producers deliberately withheld supplies *and* when the industrial nations were in the middle of an arduous winter *and* when they could not convert to other sources of energy. If alternative energy sources are developed, oil will no longer be a strategic resource in international economies. If considerably less energy can be consumed, then oil will lose its strategic value as a power resource, but, until then, it is going to be a dominant strategic power resource that can be used to induce or coerce nations to do the OPEC countries' bidding.

To summarize then, the key concept to bear in mind concerning possession of resources as a power base is that such resources must be *applicable* to the situation and it must be difficult to convert other resources to the strategic resource without delays or great costs. Finally, the power resource need not be materials. Such things as a pool of quality management talent or R and D skills could be important power resources.

However, there is another facet to the structure of resources, and that is in the structure of alternatives. This is discussed next.

CONTROL OF ALTERNATIVES

This section can be introduced by a hypothetical situation.

- Suppose there is one person in the entire country who is qualified to carry out a certain job. Suppose also that there is only one organization that needs the qualifications of this person but that they *really* need him in order to operate.

The question then is who has the power in this situation. The answer is that the person and the organization *both* have power over one another. The person can do a great deal of harm to the organization by not cooperating, so he has the basis for coercion by the fact that he possesses unique skills that are desired by the organization. At the same time, the organization has a basis of coercion in that it is uniquely needed as a place of employment for the skilled person.   So they both have power, but it tends to be balanced.

What happens when there are *two* people with these skills and only *one* organization?   We sense immediately that the organization has more power than either of the individuals, because it has more alternatives than they do. Unless the individuals can get together and form a coalition (which will be discussed later), which then reduces the alternatives available to the organization, the organization can induce or coerce one or both of the individuals to do its bidding far more easily than in the case of the one-to-one relationship.

We can, therefore, argue that the structures of alternatives available to an organization and its opponents are important determinants of power.   The more alternatives an organization has available *relative* to its opponents, the more power it has.

Going back to the crude oil situation, it was only when the OPEC countries got together and formed a united bloc that they succeeded in wresting the power from their customers.   Since the oil-purchasing countries appear to be incapable of forming an effective counterbody to reduce the alternative structure more to their favor, this situation is likely to persist.   Moreover, it is often the *marginal* impact of an alternative that is important.   For instance, consider the situation illustrated in Figure 2.5.

Figure 2.5 Effect of Marginal Alternatives on a Power Structure

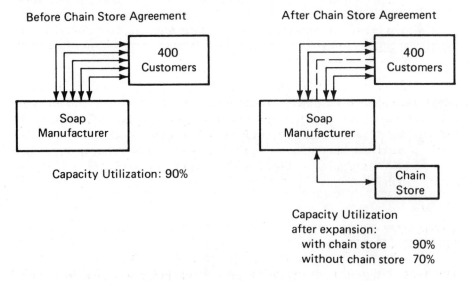

- A certain small soap manufacturer was producing and selling fancy soap to 400 customers when it was approached by a large chain store and asked to provide soap for the chain under its brand name. At that point, it was operating at 90 percent of capacity, and the contract offered by the chain store was in the region of 25 percent of capacity. The offer looked very good, and the company went ahead and expanded capacity by 30 percent (the smallest feasible expansion for a new plant). After one year of operation with the new plant, the chain store demanded a substantial reduction in its contract price. Despite the fact that the manufacturer had *400 alternatives*, the impact of losing the chain store contract would have been disastrous; instead of operating at about 90 percent of capacity, they would have been operating at about 70 percent of capacity, which would have brought them well below break-even with the new fixed cost structure. The soap company had been outmaneuvered in this case due to the *marginal impact* of the chain store alternative.

Therefore, analysis of the alternative structures should consider the marginal impacts of alternatives.

INFLUENCE AS A SOURCE OF POWER

Often, it is possible to use influence in a situation in order to achieve a power position.

• Consider the example mentioned earlier in which a truck seat manufacturer persuaded the union to demand installation of his seats in truck bodies. The seat manufacturer did not have the power to get the truck assemblers to do as he wished, so he turned to those people who would gain the greatest benefit from the use of his truck seats. By developing influence with the union, he managed to employ *their* power to accomplish the purpose he had in mind.

Therefore, in the analysis of situations for the development of a power base, it is often useful to ask what parties there are who *do* have a power base and whether the organization can use influence with *them* to accomplish what it cannot do on its own. Thus, an insightful political analysis identifies not only the relationships that are amenable to direct manipulation but also those that are amenable to indirect manipulation.

AUTHORITY AS A SOURCE OF POWER

The fact that one has authority in a situation gives rise to opportunities for developing a power base. An individual usually is given authority to accomplish some purpose. The fact that an individual has the authority to do it confers on him a mantle of formal legitimacy that opponents may not have. In such situations, the individual has an edge over an opponent who is not accepted as having formal authority.

● Have you ever wondered why some people are on so many committees that appear to be extremely boring and tedious? Being on the committee often confers on them some legitimate authority as members of that committee. This situation was particularly relevant in an industry committee that was formed to talk to the government on new regulations. Members of the industry were asked to form a committee on regulation, and there was much jockeying by companies that wanted to be selected for the committee. Each company recognized that only a few companies would be represented and that these companies then would have the authority to speak *for the industry as a whole.*

BASES OF INFLUENCE

Here, we are concerned with the ways a political actor may change *perceptions* of his opponents, rather than changing the situation itself.

POSSESSION OF STRATEGIC INFLUENCING RESOURCES

In order to change perceptions, the influencer must undertake a communication process. This means that, in order for him to gain influence, certain resources must be at his disposal. First, the actor must be *able to communicate* with the influencers. Second, the influencees must be *prepared to accept* the communication. Third, they must *believe* the communication. Fourth, the influencer must have some *knowledge of the value systems* of the influencees. Fifth, the influencer must possess *information that is relevant* to the situation and to the influencees. Sixth, the influence depends upon the *structure of commitments* that already exist on the part of the influencees, as well as the strength of these commitments.

These six requirements determine the kinds of resources that are necessary for the exercise of influence in any situation. It is convenient to categorize these resources into three broad classes of strategic influence resources: audience, information, and commitments.

Audience

The extent to which the influencer can physically communicate with the influencees; the rapport that he can establish with them on the basis of knowledge of their values, and their propensity for receiving and paying attention to the influence effort, based on their perception of his prestige, credibility, reliability and expertise.

Development of communication systems and credibility structures and knowledge of the value system of the opponents are very costly. Resources deployed to develop audience often must be diverted from other purposes, such as development of a power base. Where attention in the literature is given to development of audience, it is generally in such areas as marketing and public relations, and it tends to ignore the need for developing audience with other important strategic stakeholders, such as banks, shareholders, government officials, competitors, and so on. Thus, inadequate attention to necessary communication systems and kinds of knowledge and credibility that are required result.

- Perhaps the best glaring example of this is reported by Lederer and Burdick (1958) in their factual epilogue. Apparently the U. S. economic mission once delivered a large consignment of tractors to Pakistan. Within days it was commonly accepted in the countryside that Russia had sent the tractors. Local communists had stenciled a red hammer and sickle on every flat surface of every tractor! All the audience and credibility that went with the large economic investment was captured for the cost of a few cans of red paint (and the creative application of the concepts of influence we are discussing here).

- Another business example was the case of an insurance company that was spending a great deal of effort attracting shareholders with public relations and advertising efforts on radio, television, and the press. Analysis revealed that over 70 percent of its shares were held by institutions such as pension funds and churches and that a substantial proportion of the funds it was deploying could have been far more effectively deployed in developing small teams of people geared specifically to cultivating such investors. In fact, after a more detailed analysis of the influence process, this was recognized and implemented, with substantial improvement in results at about one-half the expenditure.

Information

As Pettigrew (1973), among others, points out the second type of resource that is required for effective influence is information that is strategically relevant to the influence attempt. This is the key information that is required if changes in the perception of the influences are to be accomplished.

- For instance, while my current influence attempt may be moderately successful (you have read this far!), if I changed the nature of the information I am bringing to you and started writing about food consumption patterns in a medieval monastery, I am sure that I soon would lose the attention of many who have stuck with me so far. The kind of information I would be bringing to bear on your perceptions would not be relevant either to your value systems or to the influence attempt at hand—the development of political strategy.

Developing information that is relevant to the situation requires analysis and insight, just as in the case of audience. A trade-off must be made, then, not only between resources that are to be deployed to developing a power base or to developing an influence base, but also *within* the influence system between resources deployed to developing audience and resources deployed to developing strategic information via intelligence systems. These intelligence systems keep in touch with the value systems and supply strategic information necessary to maintain the interest and attention of the influencees.

Commitments

The final general resource that is important in an influence system is commitments. People commit themselves in two ways, to principles and to other actors.

- For instance, business people may be committed to *principles* relating to the *value systems they hold* (such as not doing business with foreign countries that espouse certain political beliefs) or to *ways of conducting business*, (such as never giving discounts, never accepting under-the-counter deals, and so on).
- Alternatively, they may be committed to people in the form of formal or informal agreements. The commitment of Japanese employers to providing lifetime job security to employees is an example. A commitment to fulfill a certain contract is another example.

Commitments can be regarded as voluntary reductions of alternatives. By committing themselves, either to principles or to people, actors automatically reduce the alternative courses of action available to them.

The extent to which the opponents have commitments has an important effect on the success of the influence attempt. In the first place, the commitment structure of the opponents is the fundamental process whereby the influencer can activate their sense of obligation.

If he can argue successfully that a course of action contemplated by the opponents is in conflict with their commitments, then he has a chance of succeeding in preventing them from carrying out that action. Second, if he can somehow get the opponents committed to himself, the ability to prevent an action that is unsuitable to him is further enhanced.

- An example in which the structure of commitments played a key role in an influence process occurred in the case of many companies faced with the Arab blacklisting of organizations doing business with Israel. Many companies that wanted Arab-world business were forced to forego this business because of existing commitments to Israel.

Therefore, a careful analysis of the structure of commitments is an important prerequisite for the effectiveness of an influence play and it may be vital to deploy resources toward developing commitments of key actors in the situation before any move is made.

It is important to recognize that influence resources, like power resources, are considered strategic only when they are *relevant* to the situation, and it takes time and effort to acquire them.

CONTROL OF ALTERNATIVES

As in the case of power, the extent to which the alternatives available in the influence system can be controlled is a major determinant of the infuence base. If an individual (or an organization) is the only actor that has an effective communications system, or credibility, or the strategic information necessary for the influencees, it will monopolize the influence process. To the extent that its opponents also have communication systems or credibility, however, its influence is reduced. If it is the only source of information, then influencees are heavily dependent on it. If it is the sole recipient of commitments, it can monopolize the obligation process. Moreover, its opponents' commitment structures are also of relevance. To the extent that they are committed to principles or people they reduce their own alternatives.

- A large travel company publically committed itself to a policy of guaranteeing to undercut the lowest prices in the market, in order to put pressure on a smaller competitor. The smaller competitor responded by drastically cutting prices in their *competitor's* key sales area. Traditional customers of the larger company went to it demanding that the price of the smaller company be undercut. The smaller company had many fewer inquiries in that area, and the people making inquiries were told that it was "a good time to take up the larger company's offer." As a result, the larger company was compelled to send many tours out considerably below cost, and in trying to economize disaffected a substantial proportion of its customers.

- At one stage, a large number of companies in the textile industry were on the verge of collapse or had collapsed. One member of the industry was a private company that was in fairly sound shape but was being encumbered by the image of the industry as a whole. Suppliers were loath to supply, investors' confidence was low, and customers were expressing concern that the orders they placed would not be delivered. The chairman of the sound company decided that he would have to differentiate the company from others in the industry if his company were to have credibility. When the next company in the industry went into voluntary liquidation, he made a publically announced bid for the failing company. If his bid had been accepted, he would have been able to resell at a modest profit. The offer was not accepted, but the fact that the offer was *made* boosted confidence in his company within days, and, for a considerable period after that, he had no trouble with suppliers or customers, most of whom were keen to do business with him *rather than anyone else*, because he had established a unique credibility in the industry. Interestingly enough, this was accomplished at absolutely no cost to his company, demonstrating the effectiveness of creative application of political action in a business context.

These examples were intended to demonstrate some of the facets of the control of influence resources. A careful analysis of the structure of such alternatives is often difficult because of the intangibility of factors such as degree of commitment and level of credibility, but this should enhance, rather than detract, from the need to take them specifically into consideration before a strategic move is launched.

POWER AS A
SOURCE OF INFLUENCE

Influence also can be obtained by the use of power, with an indirect approach. If a person (or an organization) does not have influence in a situation involving an opponent but has power over another party who does have influence, it may be possible to induce the third party to exert his influence. This is particularly important in situations in which the person to be influenced steadfastly rejects any attempts or overtures at persuasion or obligation on the part of the influencer. In these situations, the necessary audience is absent and the influence seeker is compelled to turn to parties who *do* have audience. When one thinks about it, these types of situations occur frequently in organizations.

- In the U. S., some companies are starting to commission reputable public opinion surveyors to test the public sentiment on issues involving regulation, particularly if these issues appeared to be spearheaded by a vociferous and well-organized, but minor, interest group. These companies know that there is no way that they *themselves* can *credibly* argue that the majority of the voters disagree—their self-interest is too evident. Hence they "buy" the credibility of reputable pollsters.

AUTHORITY AS A SOURCE OF INFLUENCE

Here, the same arguments that applied to power as a source of influence apply, since authority is conceived as legitimized power *and* influence. Refer to the section on authority as a source of power.

SUMMARY: KEY CONCEPTS

In this chapter, a number of simplifications have been made. No attention was given to the *capability* of the persons to recognize their power/influence in a situation, nor to their adeptness at exercising their political capability. The discussion was carried out as if persuasion, obligation, inducement, and coercion could be carried out in a pure form, when, in fact, a mix of these means of manipulation is used usually in practice.

Manipulation has been discussed as if it were a unilateral action on the part of the manipulator, when, in fact, the opponent may be making countermoves and when, in fact, the opponent and the manipulator could be negotiating a joint agreement *while* the manipulative action is taking place. To take a simple case, a manipulator may negotiate with his opponent the size of the inducement to be given for the manipulator to be successful. It is only for conceptual convenience that the process of manipulation is discussed as it if were separate from other types of political action.

The key points from this chapter are these.

1. Power can be conceived of as the capacity of an actor to restructure a situation so that his opponents will act as he desires.

2. Influence can be conceived of as the capacity of an actor to restructure the opponent's perceptions of situations, so that they will act as he desires.

3. Authority may be regarded as legitimized political capability (that is, power plus influence).

4. Strategic power resources, control of alternatives, influence, and authority are major bases of power in a situation.

5. Strategic influence resources, control of alternatives, power, and authority are major bases of influence in a situation.

6. Both power and influence are situationally determined; that is, having power and influence in one situation does not necessarily mean having power and influence in another.

7. Effective political strategies can only be evolved from a careful analysis of the power and influence *potential* of the situation. In this case difficult trade-offs must be made between deployment of resources to develop power and/or influence in the situation.

3

Negotiation

THE CONCEPT OF NEGOTIATION

By *negotiation*, we mean a situation in which two or more actors whose interests are in conflict come to some kind of joint agreement about how they will behave with respect to *one another*.

Coalition formation occurs when two or more actors get together and agree on joint action with respect to yet other actors. This will be discussed in the next chapter.

So, if Able goes to Charlie and demands a salary increase, and, after some discussion, they agree on an increase, we are talking about negotiation. However, if Able and Baker get their heads together as to how they are both going to approach Charlie for an increase, then Able and Baker are forming a coalition before they negotiate with Charlie.

Most of the most important fundamental concepts of negotiation have been extremely well explored by various authors. In this chapter, a great deal of the argument is based on a few key works by Schelling (1963), Walton and McKersie (1969), Karass (1970) and Kennedy (1965). There is no hope of being able to cover these works in depth in a single chapter, and I strongly encourage the reader to explore these concepts further by starting with the references at the back of the book.

Walton and McKersie point out that there are several types of nego-tiation that can occur between opponents. First, they could negotiate what share of the profits each party will take. This is called *distribu-tive bargaining,* much like arguing what "share of the pie" each party will get. Second, they could negotiate how to *increase* profits (and *then* perhaps what share each will take). This is called *integrative bargaining* (something like negotiating "how to make the pie bigger"). Third, each party could be carrying out tactics geared at changing the attitudes of their opponents, making the opponents more or less hos-tile. This is called *attitude structuring.* Finally, if they are *repre-sentatives* of other groups, they could be deciding how to persuade their respective constituents that the agreement they are reaching is an acceptable one. This is called *intraorganizational negotiation.*

In this chapter, we will confine ourselves primarily to the case of *distributive bargaining,* not because the other types of negotiation are not important, but because space is just not available to handle them all and the distributive bargaining process is the one that is allied most closely to the deliberate political perspective of this book.

To introduce the concepts of negotiation, let us take a simple case of a person, called Seller wishing to sell a small business.

Karass points out that there appear to be two limits to the kind of deal that Seller might make. First, there is a lower limit below which Seller will not sell the business at all. This is Seller's *bargaining base.* If Seller gets an offer anywhere below this base, the deal is impossible. Second, there is a less obvious but important *upper limit* that Seller feels will be the best possible price he can hope to get. This is Seller's *aspiration base,* which Seller doesn't really expect to have exceeded under even the best circumstances. Suppose Seller's aspiration base and bargaining base are as depicted in Figure 3.1.

Figure 3.1. Seller's Aspiration and Bargaining Bases.

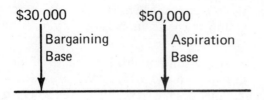

Then suppose that Seller decided to place an advertisement offering his business for sale in the local newspaper. If you were Seller, what price would you ask for the business? In most Western societies, people are inclined to put up an initial offer on, or above, the aspiration base with the expectation that they will have to move down. This is *not* necessarily true in other societies, however.

For the sake of simplicity, let us suppose that Seller's initial offer is at his aspiration base, and the business goes on the market at $50,000. Suppose then that a person called Buyer is interested in the business. He too will have an aspiration base, in his case the *lowest price* that he thinks he will be able to pay for the business, and a bargaining base, in this case the highest price he is prepared to pay for the business. These bases are as depicted in Figure 3.2.

Figure 3.2. Buyer's Aspiration and Bargaining Bases.

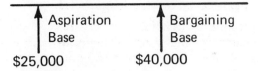

If Buyer follows the expected pattern, he will make an initial offer that is equal to, or lower, than his aspiration base. Let us suppose that his first offer is at his aspiration base. If we put the two figures together (always remembering that neither Seller nor Buyer know their opponent's bases), then we get Figure 3.3.

Figure 3.3. Buyer and Seller Combined.

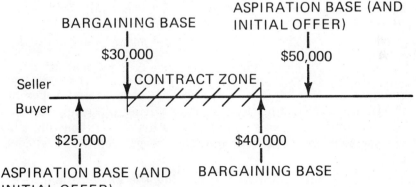

Immediately, we can see several things from Figure 3.3. First, unless the two bargaining bases overlap to form a contract zone, there can be no deal. If a deal is going to be struck, it will be somewhere in the contract zone between $30,000 and $40,000. Second, if Seller's initial price is $50,000 and Buyer's is $25,000, then, obviously, one of them must make a concession if a deal is to go through at all. Schelling argues that *neither* will make a concession as long as they both think the other might make a concession. If this is correct, then some interesting implications emerge. For, if Seller *cannot* find some way of locking himself into the $50,000 and Buyer *can* lock himself into the $25,000, then, unless Seller has an alternative buyer, he will find that he has to make a concession or the negotiation will deadlock.

The reverse applies to Buyer. Therefore, both parties have to find a lock; yet if they both *do*, then *neither* can move. If both cannot find ways of locking themselves into their offer, then the one who cannot will find himself being pulled to his bargaining base.

The process whereby they find ways of sticking to their current offers is the essence of Schelling's arguments about distributive bargaining.

THE BLUFF

THE NATURE OF THE BLUFF

Each negotiator must try to bluff and make it seem that his *current* offer is his *last* offer. In order for this bluff to succeed, each must find a way of *committing* himself to his bluff. Unless Seller can commit himself in some way to his offer of $50,000, Buyer will drag Seller's price down.

Thus, bluff tactics involve developing a set of commitments to each offer, that attempts to persuade the opponent that this offer is really the last one. What we need to consider is the nature and implications of these commitments.

In the first place, Seller needs to be aware that Buyer is *also* committing himself to *his* bluff. If the deal looks good and Seller has committed himself too firmly to the current offer and it appears that Buyer has committed himself completely to his offer, then they may find themselves in deadlock, even though a very acceptable deal could be made.

Therefore, it is important in formulating the bluff to make sure that the negotiator has a loophole by which he can get *out* of the commitment, if necessary. If he has this loophole, then he can allow his opponent to talk him out of the commitment, or he can even talk himself out of it. So, the commitment is not a simple case of formulating some unequivocal reason why one cannot budge and then sticking to it.

What usually happens then is that both parties formulate commitments to their current offers, bluffing that these are their last offers, and then they try to persuade their opponents that the other's commitment is not final. When one party is convinced that the opponent will not concede, he allows himself to be talked out of his current commitment and makes a new offer. Typically, but not necessarily, what also happens is that opponents start with moderately low commitments and these increase as they move toward their bargaining base.

However, a real danger arises if they both increase their commitments as they get closer to their bargaining bases, because there is the peculiar situation that the closer they get to an increasingly desirable deal for both, the greater the danger of deadlock! At times like this, there is a great pressure to release the tension and accept the opponent's offer, at the negotiator's own expense.

Having discussed the nature of bluffing, it is perhaps useful to consider some of the tactics that can be employed in bluffing. Here again, extensive use is made of Schelling's insights.

BLUFF TACTICS

What is presented here is a list of general tactics that can be employed in bluffing. The creative talents of the reader must be employed to fit the general tactics to the specific negotiation he faces. Bluffs involve formulating a commitment to a current offer. Schelling has identified a number of such tactics. This list is by no means exhaustive, but it covers the most common bluff tactics.

COMMITMENT TO A DEADLINE IN ABSENCE OF COMMUNICATION

- A property seller sent a signed contract by messenger to a potential client with a letter containing the following message, "I have decided that $50,000 is the lowest offer I can possibly accept. I am enclosing a contract to that effect because, unfortunately, I am leaving for Chicago on urgent business. I am very sorry, but, if you haven't signed the contract by 5 p. m. today, I'll have to consider the deal off. There is nothing more I can do, I have just run out of time. I hope it works out." (The contract was signed by the buyer.)

If this tactic works, how does it work? Basically, the property dealer in this situation made a final offer and committed himself by setting a deadline and breaking off communication until the deadline had passed. If the deal looks good to the opponent, then the opponent has no choice but to accept the offer *or* find some way of reestablishing communication *or* let the deal slip through his hands.

Thus, creative use of deadlines, even ones artificially introduced into the situation, together with creative ways of breaking off or preventing communication, can be employed in formulating bluff tactics.

THE NATURE OF TACTICS

The first thing that we should note about the tactic just discussed (and all tactics) is that it is *not riskless*. The property dealer ran the risk that the contract would not be signed. In the case described, he judged right and the opponent did sign. However, the opponent said later that, if the property dealer had asked for $55,000, he would not have signed. Every tactic discussed below has the characteristics that are sought in order to gain greater reward by increasing risk. The easiest thing the tactician can do is to accept his opponent's initial offer, but this is costly, even though it is riskless. The highest reward is to stick firmly to an initial offer, but then the negotiator runs the risk of having the deal fall through. The negotiator has to use his judgment to decide what reward he wants to shoot for and at what risk.

The second thing to note about this tactic is that it *is* a tactic; that is, it is a single play in a more complex strategy in which a number of tactics are employed to fit the overall direction the negotiator wishes to take. Because tactics are less complex, they are also more visible and therefore can be recognized. This gives rise to two problems. The first is that the opponent can anticipate tactics which are used too often. The property dealer would have to be careful not to use the same tactic (for a while, at least) if he were doing a number of deals with the same buyer and not to get known in the market as a user of that particular tactic. If he used the tactic too often, the opponent could develop counter-tactics.

The second problem with using the same tactic with the same people too frequently is that even if negotiator does win, they start getting emotionally upset with it and forget the rational solution in their haste to "get even," even if it means the deal has to fall through. Therefore, it is appropriate to use a *mix* of tactics in a negotiation.

The point that is being made here is this: *if the negotiator does not plan a negotiation beforehand, he has less chance of success than if he does.*

COMMITMENT TO A THIRD PARTY

- The essence of this tactic is the negotiator's seeming commitment to a third party, so that he runs the risk of punishment if he does not stick to his offer. Then, it is not his fault that he is being so obstinate!

- The boss of a small company was faced perenially with the problem of a valuable supplier (of whom the company was a valuable customer) who every year demanded a 10-percent increase in material prices. On one particular year, the boss went to his board and asked them for a directive demanding that he not accept any price increases "due to the profit erosionary impact of inflation." He used this document to persuade his opponent that it was only at risk to his position that he could give the supplier a 3-percent increase. (The two parted on good terms.)

USE OF A LACKEY

- The chief of a data-processing service company used to send out his sales-people with explicit and very demanding instructions when they were closing data-processing contracts with clients. They were given written, explicit instructions as to what prices, guarantees, and terms to meet. Whenever the client made a demand, the salesperson would check the in-structions and indicate whether the demand fitted his instructions. If the client continued the demand, the salesperson would promise to return after checking with the boss. On return, a slightly modified position would be presented. On the relatively few occasions when the sales-person was dismissed by the client, then and only then would the boss take over the negotiations.

This is a very important tactic. In the first place, the boss may have *too much* authority. After all, the boss *is* the boss and can be subjected to demands from an opponent that would be unthinkable to demand from a subordinate. Thus, it is a way of restricting authori-ty to make concessions. Second, it sets out the ballpark in which the game will be played. Before the main protagonists get together, they must make sure that they have, to some extent, signaled ahead of time some limits on the concessions that will be demanded of them. Third, it is a way of softening up the opponent. Fourth, it provides an op-portunity of seeing how tough-minded the opponent is, and allows the negotiator to assess his strengths and weaknesses before he exposes himself.

USE OF AN AGENT

Instead of negotiating himself, an individual (or an organization) might employ a professional negotiator to act for him. He should take care that he structures the reward of his agents in such a way that the reward they receive is commensurate with how well they do for him, and not for just closing the deal.

The point is that many professional negotiators are rewarded just for closing the deal—by providing the right incentives, the individual employing agents may be able to get them to focus on driving a good deal for him.

COMMITMENT TO THE PUBLIC

- Prior to a round of labor contract negotiations, union leaders published in their press the fact that they were going to get at least a fifty-cent-per-hour increase for their members. When the negotiations got underway, they could argue convincingly that their reputation and credibility with the membership would be destroyed if they accepted any less.

The major point about bluff tacts is that they should be *convincing*. The union's opponents were placed in the awkward position of finding ways (via concessions on other issues) of making *any* concession by the union on wages look less damaging.

If one can find a way of communicating a bluff to an interested audience one is committed to keeping it.

COMMITMENT TO PRINCIPLE/POLICY

- A chemicals company uses the following argument in negotiations with customers: "It is 'against our policy' to give discounts for large volume. This would give the larger companies a competitive edge over their smaller competitors, who have supported us for many years." Since the company's products are of high quality, they are able to get away with this commitment.

  Commitment to policy or principles are rather easy to invoke and have the advantage that they are extremely difficult to subvert. If one tries to attack a commitment to principles, the implications are that the principles of the opponent are in doubt. If one tries to attack a commitment to policy, one finds it difficult to get back to the amorphous source of that policy.

COMMITMENT TO PRECEDENT

- A common argument in labor negotiations is that, if one concedes this year, one will have to concede next year as well. A concession would set a precedent for later negotiations, and one cannot afford to set that precedent. (Then, it is up to the opponent to persuade the negotiator that this is not the case.)

- A manufacturer of quality chrome tube furniture refuses to make special orders on the argument that, if he makes special orders for one, he will have to make it for all the other customers, and this would drive his costs up.

If one can argue convincingly that a concession sets a precedent for negotiations *over time* or *across many opponents*, one has a very strong argument for not conceding.

COMMITMENT TO AN OPPONENT VIA A THIRD PARTY

- A chemical company was trying to license a new product from an overseas patent holder. The patent-holding company sent two negotiators, one of whom was particularly obstinate, unreasonable, and obnoxious. Some time after the negotiations were started, the obnoxious person was "called away" and the second member of the team confessed that he was very uncomfortable with his colleague. He persuaded the representatives of the chemical company that, if they could come to a quick settlement just below what his unconceding colleague was demanding, he could get his colleague to accept it.

If the situation can be structured in such a way that one can "commit" oneself to one's opponent in the face of conflict with a third party, then the third party bears the brunt of the blame for being unyielding and unreasonable, while one appears to be sympathetic and rational.

COMMITMENT VIA OBSTINACY

It is possible that by sheer obstinacy (feigned or not), one can convince the opponents that whatever their arguments, one is not going to move from one's offer.

INVOKING AN ALTERNATIVE

A very common method of commitment is to claim that one has an alternative offer.

- An antique dealer would try to arrange for one of the potential purchasers to call him while he was having an appointment with another client interested in the same piece. (He never had fake calls made.) This was a nerve-shattering demonstration by the antique dealer that more than one alternative was available.

PLAYING FOR TIME

As a counter to an opponent's commitment, when the negotiator does not have a ready commitment for his bluff, there are a variety of ways playing for time.

Postponement

Finding a plausible way of postponing the negotiation is a useful ploy, which should be prepared beforehand so that one doesn't have to use a spurious reason to break it off.

Feigning Misunderstanding

If one is somehow unable to understand an opponent's commitments, one can gain time.

- On one occasion, an executive who was faced with a demand for rate increases in the travel industry calculated the cost structure five times, each time getting a different answer. He then said that perhaps he better sit down with his accountant and work things out. This gave him time to develop a countertactic.

Raising Another Issue

Since few negotiations are about a single issue, such as price, it is often possible to turn to another issue and argue that while playing for time on the current issue. [This is a favorite ploy of politicians who are in a corner.]

Nitpicking

It is sometimes possible to start picking apart the precise nature of the opponent's bluff, trying to raise a dust cloud over minor points while the major point is being obscured. This is a favorite ploy of many attorneys.

Obviously, there are many more tactics that can be employed, but most of the main ones have been covered. Let us, therefore, turn to the next type of tactical move, the threat.

THE THREAT

THE NATURE OF THE THREAT

• The soap company described in chapter 2, after it had installed the extra capacity to support the contract with the chain store, was faced with the following demand when the contract was to be renegotiated: "We want a reduction of 15 percent in price or we will take our business to your competitor."

• A small toy-manufacturing company was operating on a fairly heavy bank overdraft when a credit squeeze took place in the economy. Banks started calling for reductions in overdrafts. After several demands from the bank, the owner of the small company went to the bank manager with the following statement: "In six months, my cash flows will turn around as I hit my seasonal selling peaks. Until then, I will have to continue an overdraft. I will not reduce it, I have inventory to build up. Either leave me alone for six months or foreclose on me. My way you get your money back in full—if you foreclose, you will get about sixty cents on the dollar. Take it or leave it." (The bank left him alone and put pressure on other companies.)

What is happening here? In each case, a threat is involved. The threatener demands certain action on the part of the target of the threat and lays out the conditions that will prevail if that action is not followed. Yet, the threats are different. The chain store stood to lose by being inconvenienced by a disruption of supply while new sources were set up, but they stood to lose far less than the soap manufacturer. This is what is called a *strong threat*—both parties lose, but the one that makes the threat loses less.

In the case of the toy manufacturer, both parties stood to lose, but the threatener stood to lose much more—his business would be closed down. This is a *weak threat*—the threatener stands to lose more than the target.[1]

The problem with a weak threat is that it is often hard to believe that the threatener will actually carry out the threat, since this is irrational. Thus, weak threats are suspect and tend to be ignored by most negotiators. However, let us explore the nature and purpose of the threat a little more clearly. What is the purpose of the threat? Obviously it is to get the opponent to do something they would rather not. Is the threat made to be successful or to fail? Obviously, negotiators don't make threats that they expect to fail. Then, if one formulates a successful threat, does one get hurt? Ob-

---

[1] A situation in which the aggressor does not get hurt at all would not be regarded as a threat. It would be coercion—"making an offer that can't be refused."

viously not, because there is no need to carry out the action that would have hurt—the opponent has behaved as was desired and there is no need for punitive action at all! Who would be hurt more then becomes academic—*neither is hurt.*

So the weak threat, as well as the strong threat, is a viable tactic, provided that the negotiator can convince his opponent that he is prepared to carry out the threat.

The way that the negotiator persuades his opponent that he intends to carry out the threat is to *commit* himself to carrying it out. A threat is nothing other than a *conditional bluff.* So in formulating threats, we are back to the whole problem of commitment again. The same type of tactics that we discussed under this topic of bluffs applies and the same problem of finding a loophole applies. In the case of the treat, however, the loophole is even more critical. Particularly with the weak threat, it is important to recognize that one's opponents know that, if one stops to act rationally when they have transgressed, one will not carry out the threat. Therefore, it is very important that the threat is carefully spelled out to indicate exactly what the transgressive act is (if it is not, while one is deciding whether the opponent has transgressed, one has time to rationalize the threat) and that the threatener does not allow the opponents to spot a loophole or they will transgress and provide the loophole for the threatener. In fact, a really good threat would appear to the opponent to be one that is automatically carried out, and the decision to carry out the threat should appear to be *out of the threatener's hands* entirely.

- An example illustrating the concept of having the threat removed from the control of the threatener occurred in the travel industry. The head of a travel company chartering planes during the 1973 oil crisis decided that the arbitrary price increases being announced by the airline from which he was chartering had to be slowed down. When the next price increase was about to be announced, he wrote to them stating that the possible 10-percent increase was too high and that, unless the airline held it at 5 percent, he would have to cancel all the tours he had arranged for the next year. He further stated that, since he would have to be away when the contract was due to be signed, he was signing and forwarding a contract to the airline. If they were not prepared to accept it, they were to notify his administrative manager, who had instructions then to cancel all tours associated with the airline in question. The head of the travel company would not be available for further discussions, since he was about to depart for a series of highly confidential negotiations in the Far East and Africa.

By structuring the threat so that it appeared to be automatically executed, he removed all opportunity for the use of his own discretion should the airline transgress. As a matter of interest, we see many of the elements of the bluff tactics which were discussed above. In this case, there was a deadline, and he found a way of committing himself to the bluff via a lackey (his administrative manager) and of communicating his commitment and then breaking off communication until the deadline passed. It was also a weak threat, because the damage to his business would have been greater than the loss of his business to the airline. (However, from the point of view of the airline, his business was important). He succeeded in holding them to a 5-percent increase, but, more important, he succeeded in putting the brakes on the automatic price increase pattern that had started emerging.

Finally, while it *appeared* to the opponents that the threat would be automatically carried out, this was not the case. If the airline *had* transgressed, the loophole that had been planned involved the lackey frantically calling the head of the airline to say that he had been instructed to cancel all tours and then being "persuaded" to hold off until the boss returned. The boss upon returning would call the airline and furiously demand to know why his subordinate had been "subverted," and, thus, he would reopen the channels of communication and the negotiations would proceed.

It is important to recognize, from this example, the urgent need, once the threat has not succeeded, for *both* parties to find some way of avoiding the execution of the threat. Thus, the commitment to a threat is much more tricky then the commitment to a bluff. It must appear that the threat *is* going to be carried out, yet there must be a *credible* loophole that will put off the execution of the threat. Otherwise, the threatener might find himself firmly committed to doing something that is extremely harmful to himself.

In addition to bluffs and threats, there is still one more negotiating tactic of great importance to be discussed before we can turn attention to negotiating strategy—this is the *promise*.

THE PROMISE

- Every now and then, the airlines agree to some kind of "no-frills" fare structure whereby the passengers are loaded into the plane and transported to their destinations without any fancy meals, movies, and so on. Then, inexorably, one after the other, the frills are reintroduced and the costs skyrocket again. Why should this happen?

- A large number of companies spew thousands of tons of effluents into the Great Lakes. Everyone deplores the impact on the environment, yet no one does anything about it. It takes very punitive federal laws to slow the pollution, when it is slowed at all. Why is this the case?

Both of these, and many other situations that require an agreement between competitors, requires a *promise*. A promise is required in a situation in which joint agreement is necessary for the good of all participants, but, if one participant does not cooperate or agrees to cooperate and then cheats, then this participant gains an advantage over the others.[2]

If the airlines all agree to no-frills flights but one gives a meal or a movie, then the passengers go to them, so all end up giving meals and movies and so on. If one industry decides not to pollute, it makes little difference to the Great Lakes, so everyone pollutes because no one can get *everyone* not to do so. In both these situations, *everyone loses out*, because they cannot promise one another not to cheat.

Basically, in order to create a successful promise, the participants have to find ways of committing themselves to a course of action even when there is an incentive to cheat. And the more everyone is persuaded that the others will not cheat, the greater the incentive for *them* to cheat. Using this reasoning about others, all opponents rationalize that they may as well cheat, so everyone loses. So, for a promise to be effective, certain conditions *must* be met. First, it must be possible to *monitor* cheaters; that is to say, a system of checking and catching cheaters must be available. Second, it must be possible to *punish* cheaters. For, if they cannot be punished, they will cheat anyway. This means that, in the absence of a monitoring system or some kind of legal or pseudo-legal system for punishing cheats, the promise is unlikely to succeed.

- An example of this occurred in the case of a cartel (in a country where cartels are not illegal.) Several companies were trying to form a price cartel but could not do so because, every time price agreements were made, the companies would go out and make under-the-counter price deals with the customers. The cartel only stabilized when the companies came to agreement on a *market-share* arrangement. Each company agreed to a certain market share. A market research organization was employed to determine market share each month, and, if one company sold more than its share, it was required to pay a penalty into a pool that was used to refund those who sold less than the agreed market share. So a means had been found both to *monitor* and to *punish* cheats. In this case, a *pseudo-legal* system had to be set up.

- In the case of the companies polluting Lake Michigan the dilemma they faced was only resolved when a superordinate body (the government) intervened to monitor and punish cheats by taking legal action against offenders. In this case, a *legal* system was set up.

[2] Technically, this sort of situation is known as a Prisoners' Dilemma.

Hence, in a situation where a promise is required, creative attention should be focused on how to develop the requisite monitoring and sanctioning systems—without them, it is fairly certain that *everyone* will end up losing.

NEGOTIATION STRATEGY

INTRODUCTION OF COMPLEXITY

So far, the discussion of negotiation has been developed along relatively simple lines. Generally, we have assumed only two individuals. Often, many individuals and groups of individuals may be involved. Also, we have assumed only one issue, such as price, but, often many issues could be at stake. We also have assumed that the parties have no alternatives, but a seller could have many potential buyers, and vice versa.

We will look at the concepts developed thus far as building blocks for more complex negotiations, in which there are more than two negotiators, more than two issues, and many alternatives.

Although many authors have addressed this situation, this discussion will be confined mostly to the approach suggested by Kennedy (1965). More detailed analyses are handled in the book by Walton and McKersie (1971) and interested readers are encouraged to pursue their interest further there. Kennedy addresses primarily three major topics: negotiation objectives, issue analysis, and negotiation planning. We will try to summarize his thinking in this section.

NEGOTIATION OBJECTIVES

In a situation of any complexity, in which there are a number of parties and issues involved, it is of fundamental importance that the negotiation be started with a clear-cut set of negotiation objectives.

- The recently promoted materials manager of a medium-sized chemical manufacturer decided to negotiate a lower price for a certain raw material. A meeting was set up, and on the morning of the meeting, he called his stores manager and the production engineer in charge of the plant that used the raw material in question. He asked them to meet him at the offices of the supplying company. The three of them sat down to discuss the matter with two representatives of the supplying company. As soon as he started discussing price, one of the supplier's managers said that price would be influenced by quality. To the materials manager's horror, his production engineer started arguing about an increase in quality. Then, the other supplier's representative said that delivery costs were increasing and that this could influence delivery performance. The materials manager really started to feel the pressure when *his* stores manager started demanding that current delivery performance not only be maintained but even improved. Somehow, he found toward the end of the negotiation that he had *four* people against him, instead of two. He eventually beat a hasty retreat after conceding a small price increase, in exchange for a number of equally small improvements in quality and delivery. In discussing the matter some weeks later, he recognized that this disastrous event was his own fault for not considering the perspectives of the people he had asked along and for not discussing the issues with them beforehand.

The point to be taken from this example is that, when many individuals are involved in a negotiation, each one of them brings with him a unique perspective that influences his stand on, and attitudes toward, the issues raised. Therefore, it is vital to know ahead of time, particularly in the case of a team of negotiators, what stand is to be taken on the issues that can be identified.

Prior to the negotiation, every attempt should be made to identify which issues are likely to arise, what the opponents are likely to demand on these issues, and which stand the negotiating team is to take on these issues. This requires an intensive issue analysis (which will be discussed in the next section), but it also implies that, before the negotiations, each team member have a clear idea of what is being sought and what compromises are acceptable. Otherwise, the team runs the danger of talking at cross purposes. In certain cases, it may even be necessary for team members who represent different interests to *prenegotiate* the stands that will be taken on each of issues. Before objectives can be set, however, a clear analysis of the issues needs to be made.

ISSUE ANALYSIS

In complex negotiations, many issues arise. The first step in any issue analysis is trying to determine ahead of time what the issues will be, so that negotiations do not become deadlocked over the unexpected appearance of an issue. In this regard, it is important to try to view the negotiation from the point of view of the opponents, as well as of the team preparing for the negotiation. Once as many issues as possible have been identified, it is useful to rank these issues in the order of importance to the negotiating team. It is in this rank-ordering process that much of the conflicts of interest *within* the team are likely to arise, thus providing the first useful product of the rank-ordering process. Rank ordering is by no means a simple process;

but the more complex the problem, the more worthwhile it is to give the matter specific attention.

• For example, Table 3.1 lists the issues that arose in the negotiation of a supplier contracting for the supply and construction of a new physical facility to a customer. The supplier was concerned first about price, then about when the completed contract would be delivered, then about payment terms and withholding clauses, then about who would manage subcontract work (the contractor or the customer), then about how design changes would be handled, then about what after-sales service would be provided, then about what performance guarantees would be provided, and finally about who would commission the plant. After having first identified the issues that would arise and what their relative importance was, it was useful to look at the *same* issues and rank order them in terms of the opponents' priorities. It would not be unusual for the order of priority in Table 3.2 to result.

Table 3.1.

Issue	Importance to Supplier
Price	1
Delivery (completion date)	2
Terms of payment	3
Control of subcontractors	4
Design changes	5
After-sales service	6
Performance guarantees	7
Commissioning	8

When he put the two sets of priorities together, we see some interesting differences in priorities (Table 3.3)

What does this mean, from the point of view of the supplier?

We see that some issues that are very important to the supplier (such as price, terms, and subcontractor control) are of much less importance to the customer, while other issues of great importance to the customer (such as guarantees and service) are of much less importance to the supplier. Finally, price is important to both, while commissioning and design changes are not very important to either. Can the supplier make any mileage out of this situation? There are

Table 3.2.

Issue	Importance to Customer
Performance guarantees	I
Delivery	II
After-sales service	III
Price	IV
Terms of payment	V
Design changes	VI
Commissioning	VII
Control of contractors	VIII

Table 3.3.

Issue	Importance to Supplier	Importance to Customer
Price	1	IV
Delivery	2	II
Terms	3	V
Subcontractors	4	VIII
Design change	5	VI
Service	6	III
Performance guarantees	7	I
Commissioning	8	VII

several very important connotations to this unsymmetrical set of priorities:

First, the fact that something is important to the customer but not to the supplier (such as performance guarantee), can be used to lever concessions out of the customer on an issue that *is* important to the supplier (such as price or terms of payment). To give in to the opponent prematurely because it is not important to you, is to lose this valuable source of leverage.

Second, the order in which issues are negotiated becomes important. Often, the first few items on the agenda are relatively unimportant to both parties. This gives the opponents a chance to test one another out and to spot weaknesses and strengths in the other's bargaining capabilities without endangering the entire negotiation. The performance of the opponents at this stage can be an important indication of their abilities, their tough-mindedness and their attitude toward the negotiation.

Third, the order in which issues are negotiated can provide useful signals for the negotiators. Supposing that the suppliers want to use their leverage on performance guarantees to lever out a better price. Then, if they can arrange to have performance guarantees placed *ahead* of price on the agenda, they can put up some very strong resistance in discussions of performance guarantees. After this resistance has been going on for some time, they can suggest that "it looks as though nothing can be done at this stage and so it might be better to return to the issue after prices have been discussed." The implications are that, if the customer gives on price, they might be prepared to give on performance guarantees. The subtle thing here is that they have only hinted at a concession; they have not made one nor promised to make one.

Finally, it is usually inappropriate to discuss an issue that is really important to both parties until other issues have been discussed and a sense of one another's strengths and weaknesses have been unfolded. The danger of deadlock tends to be highest at this early stage when important issues are discussed first. The order of issue discussion (or agenda) is so important that many negotiations are preceded by a negotiation of the agenda itself.

- In international negotiations, such as the Paris Peace Talks between the United States and North Vietnam, considerable time was devoted to negotiating *how* the negotiations were to take place. Similarly, in many labor-management negotiations, there are informal prenegotiation sessions during which the agendas are negotiated informally. Once the issues have been identified and the priorities have been assigned to them, the negotiating team is in a position to decide which stands it will take on the various issues and what its bargaining base is for each issue.

  The next stage involves determining information about the opponents. Information about the opponents *must* be obtained, if one is to anticipate their negotiating tactics. One needs to know the character of the opposing team members: Are they impulsive or rational? Are they a single bloc, or do they have different members representing different interests? Which alternatives do they have? Which resources do they have? Which tactics do they tend to employ? Does one person have the final say? Are they lackeys or principals? This type of information is needed to prepare the negotiation plan (which is discussed next).

NEGOTIATION PLAN

Given a feel for the issues and their priorities, given the objectives that will specify the stand that will be taken on each issue, we are finally in a position to discuss the negotiating plan.

The plan starts with a specification of the order in which the negotiating team would like issues to be discussed. If resistance to this order is expected, the most likely agenda is specified. Given the best of the team's knowledge about its opponents' negotiating styles, they should try to identify which bluffs, threats, and promises will be necessary for them to make. At the same time, they might try to identify the bluffs, threats, and promises that the opponent might try, so that they can prepare counterbluffs, counterthreats, and counterpromises.

Since the team goes into the negotiation with limited information about their opponents and they will learn this information as the negotiation proceeds, they should try to identify the most critical phases in the negotiation. When things start going badly or well, they need to know how important those indications are. Perhaps they even need to plan the point at which they might want to have a break in the negotiations, so that they can replan after the critical information has become available.

In very complex negotiations, it is usually useful to focus on the *key* issues and the *key* bluffs, threats, and promises that are necessary for a successful negotiation and develop a *theme* that will be the main basis of the argument. When critical points are identified, a *few* key themes might be developed. This depends upon how the team expects these critical issues to go. When issues are being discussed, the team then can keep to those themes that form the main basis for the overall negotiation.

- For instance, in the example of a chemical plant contract discussed earlier, the supplier might develop a theme that revolves around their having the most reliable processing equipment in that particular business. Sticking to this theme (which meets two of the customers' highest priority issues: guarantees and after-sales service), they can develop strong commitments to higher prices, quicker payments, and control of subcontractors. The bluffs, threats, and promises required to support their demands on these issues will then all be cast in the light of their commitment to a highly reliable plant, good after-sales service, and somewhat flexible completion dates. Any demands to reduce price can then be said to jeopardize quality of plant and service. Any demand to speed up delivery date can be argued to require additional price. So, by sticking to a specific theme, an overall thrust of the negotiation can be developed that gives the supplier's argument credibility, coherence, and consistency.

Once the negotiation plan has been formulated, it is important also to specify the major checkpoints that will be used in the program of negotiation. If, at any stage in the negotiation, these checkpoints are not achieved (and this often happens), it is a signal for the negotiator to break off, if possible, and review progress to date with the purpose of reformulating the plan.

SUMMARY: KEY CONCEPTS

1. Every negotiator enters a negotiation with a bargaining base and an aspiration base.

2. Negotiators will not concede as long as they feel that their opponents may concede.

3. To avoid having to concede, it is necessary to formulate a commitment to the current offer. This is a bluff that the current offer is the last offer.

4. A bluff should have a loophole that can be used to break a deadlock.

5. A threat is a conditional bluff, and so a weak threat can be as viable as a strong threat, provided that the commitment to carry out the threat can be demonstrated.

6. A promise is a self-commitment that opponents need to make in a situation where they can cheat.

7. For a promise to be effective, some system of monitoring and punishing cheats is necessary.

8. Negotiating strategy should start with the formulation of negotiation objectives.

9. In complex negotiations, issue analysis is necessary, particularly to determine the relative priorities of issues between opponents.

10. In formulating a negotiation plan in the face of high complexity, a major theme should be developed and pursued throughout the negotiation. Tactics can be developed to support the theme.

4

Individual Political Behavior and Coalition Formation in Organizations

Thus far, we have discussed the concepts of manipulation and negotiation. The next facet of political behavior that needs to be explored is that of coalition formation. In order to develop an understanding of coalition activity, we will first consider the political behavior of individuals in organizations. As before, a deliberately political perspective will be used. For this analysis, we will look at individual behavior in organizations in terms of the individual *acting in his own self-interest* toward other members or parts of the organization in the pursuit of his own goals. As we will see in the chapter, there are many equally valid ways of looking at individual behavior in which the deliberate political perspective is not used. Some of these other perspectives will be drawn on in our development of the theme of the argument, but only where they are appropriate to the particular perspective we wish to pursue.

This chapter starts with a discussion of the political behavior of the individual in general, and then it systematically narrows to consider the political behavior of a member of an organization.

A general model of individual political behavior is proposed. In the course of such political behavior, two types of political activity are

50

identified.   These are manipulation activity and accommodation activity.

In the following sections, the discussion turns more specifically to the behavior of individuals in *organizations*.   Individuals join, and submit to the authority of, organizations, because they hope to achieve more long-term benefits than they would by not joining.   In essence, the individual in the organization *still* carries out manipulation, bargaining, and coalition activity, but he acts not only in his own interests but sometimes in the interest of the coalitions to which he belongs, and of the organization as a whole.

INDIVIDUAL MOTIVATION

Numerous theories of motivation in the work situation have been evolved, Maslow (1954), Schein (1963), McGregor (1960), among others.   In this section, the argument is based on the contribution of Maslow (1954), who postulated a hierarchy of needs ranging from physiological needs through safety and security needs, social needs, esteem needs related to the individual's self-respect, and finally self-actualizing needs.   In accordance with his *personal* hierarchy of needs, the individual allocates his scarce resources to the attainment of these needs.   However, this allocation of resources need not be confined purely to the satisfaction of current needs but also can be attuned to the creation of conditions in his environment that will reduce the uncertainty of the future satisfaction of these needs.

If the individual perceives that the actions of others will influence the attainment of these needs, he can behave as a small political system in his own right by acting against those actors who influence his potential need satisfaction via manipulation or accommodation with them.

To explore the concept of political behavior of the individual let us turn to an example.

- Let us consider the example of an acquaintance (called Mike) who was a draftsman by training but had an intense interest in painting.   In order to provide his basic physiological needs, Mike decided to join an organization that would provide him with a salary.   However, the nature of the jobs that he could take varied enormously, and, in considering a particular job, he considered factors other than salary in terms of how he could satisfy his other needs.   He could have tried to get a job that provided challenge to his drafting ingenuity and an opportunity for promotion to a senior position; yet, he could have looked for a *less* challenging job in order to pursue his intense interest in painting.   After assessing the op-

MacMillan Strategy Form:Pol.Concepts CTB—3

portunities he perceived in his environment, he formulated a "strategy" that involved him taking a job that paid fairly well but was not demanding of his time over weekends or beyond normal working hours. This arrangement would allow him to paint. He negotiated with several employers for a job that allowed him time to pursue his interest in painting. Depending on the alternatives available to *them*, potential employers made their decisions to accept this or not. He finally entered into a role agreement with the management of a particular firm as to what he was to do in exchange for his salary. However, in the performance of this role, he found he was not finding the time he desired for painting, and he tried to restructure the situation. He looked around the organization and found other people who desired more money *or* more staff to assist them. So he tried to form a coalition with them to make demands from the management. He promised support to this group on condition that the group (or coalition) committed themselves to a demand for more *staff* rather than more *money*, since he was not interested in the money but in putting less time into the job. So, in exchange for his support, he demanded group commitment to an issue that was *strategic to him*, namely extra staff to reduce overtime. If the group had not agreed to demand more staff but had decided to demand more money instead, he would have withdrawn his support. Eventually, the group committed itself to his strategic issue. They also asked him to take a role in finding other people in his department who would support the group and to help get a petition drawn up and signed by those supporters in his department.

At the same time, Mike joined other interest groups. He joined an artists' club in order to work with, and learn from, people who had similar interests. He found that most members in this club tended to be concerned more with having exhibitions and selling their work than with helping one another develop their talents. However, he also found a group of people in the club who would have liked less emphasis placed on exhibitions and sales, and he tried to join this group. This group was pushing for other changes in the club, in which he was not interested. In exchange for his support, he demanded that they specifically commit themselves to pursuing a talent development program as well as the other changes. In coming to an agreement with them, he was asked to prepare a timetable of such talent development activities. When he did this successfully, he became the informal manager of such activities and developed authority in this regard, thus increasing his authority in the club.

From this example, we can get a sense of the processes that are described in the model that follows. Some individuals would accept their lot, both on the job and in the club, and resign themselves to the frustration of never being able to get time to paint, while others might take the more active role that Mike took and try to restructure conditions to achieve their own ends.

We are concerned here with the behavior of individuals who do not accept their lot but try to restructure their environment to achieve their ends in the face of actions by others that would influence these ends, namely, the behavior of a political individual.

ACTION OF THE POLITICAL INDIVIDUAL

The actions of a political individual could be conceived to follow the hierarchical structure depicted in Figure 4.1. (In working through the description of the model in Figure 4.1, it may be helpful to review the example we have just been through.)

The individual has values that set limits on what action he will *allow* himself to take, as well as a certain measure of political capability in his situation that sets limits on what actions he *can* take. If he is a political individual, he surveys his environment, estimates the developments in his environment, and thereby perceives certain opportunities and threats for the achievement of his own goals. Together, the extent to which he can perceive opportunities and threats and the extent of his political capabilities determine the extent of his political action. A person who does not or cannot perceive threats and opportunities may tend to operate in a far less political way than one who does. A person with very little political capability may not be able to exploit the opportunity or avert the threats that he perceives.

On the basis of his perceived opportunities and threats, the individual can evolve a personal political strategy aimed at obtaining long-term assurance that his needs will be satisfied (often subject to current need satisfactions). His actions may therefore, be directed to three types of problems: satisfaction of current needs, creation of conditions for future satisfaction of needs, and creation of political capability for future political action.

On the basis of the personal strategy that he evolves, the individual can start political action with the environment. He can mobilize his political capabilities and attempt to manipulate the situation in which he finds himself. If he does not have sufficient political capability to manipulate his whole environment, he may start accommodating,[1] to perhaps a number of people who represent political groups,

---

[1] Note that the accommodation process can be explicit or implicit. Most individuals undertake implicit bargaining and may even be unaware that bargaining is taking place, learning by trial and error what the sanction structure of their situation is.

Figure 4.1. Political Nature of Individual Action.

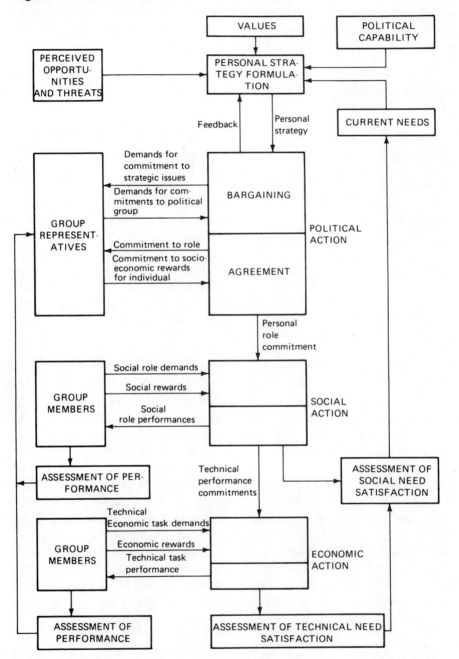

Source: "Organization Dynamics: MBL (General Management) Cycle III, Guide 3," University of South Africa, 1975. Reprinted by permission.

demanding that the group pursue certain strategic issues (for him), which, if successful, would ensure the satisfaction of his future individual needs. In the course of this negotiating, he may utilize his political capabilities to ensure the best negotiating terms for himself. In return for group commitment to his issues, the group representatives demand that the individual commit himself to political group support. As this bargaining progresses, the results of the bargaining process feed back and modify the individual's personal strategy.

Eventually, an agreement may be reached with any of a number of political groups, the terms of agreement consisting of a commitment on the part of the individual to perform certain political, social, and technical roles for the group in exchange for a commitment by the group to provide certain political, social, and economic rewards for the individual.

The results of the *political* action determine the individual's role in his *social* action involving the various groups with which he is affiliated. The group members will, in terms of the agreement, make certain social role demands on the individual. In the process of performing his role, he interacts with the group members and receives social rewards. His performance is assessed by members and fed back to the group representatives for control purposes. The social rewards the individual obtains are assessed by him and fed back to his personal strategy. If the individual is successful in his personal strategy, he can increase progressively his political capability in the situation and so become more effective politically.

Let us now look at the implications for an individual in an organization.

POLITICAL ACTION OF
INDIVIDUALS IN ORGANIZATIONS

By joining *organizations*, individuals subject themselves to the authority of the organization. After the role agreement is made, they acknowledge the right of the organization (within limits) to exercise power and influence over them. The organization as a whole can make certain binding decisions regarding the behavior of individual members and how they as individuals act for the accomplishment of the organization's goals. Individuals submit to organizational authority, because they feel that doing so improves their chances of attaining their goals. Furthermore, this submission to the authority of the organization is determined by a complex bargaining process and is contingent upon the organization's satisfying certain of the individual's goals, or at least committing itself to act in such a way that his goals will be satisfied. This bargaining process takes place via the individual's interest-group membership.

However, even once he is part of the organization, the individual may continue to act politically within the organization's political boundary and may strive continually to improve his political capability with regard to the organization and other members of the organization. Improvement of his political capability results in better terms for him and also ensures his long-term need satisfaction.

While he remains a member of the organization, the individual can act politically in three ways:

1. He can act as his own agent. He can act to increase his own political capability in the organization and in his interest groups.

2. He can act as the agent of his interest groups. He can act to increase the political capability of his own interest groups, *provided* this increase in political capability does not detract from his own, in which case he may resist.

3. He can act as an agent of the organization. He can act to increase the political capability of the organization as a whole, to ensure its survival and success, and to support any proposed action that will improve the organization's status, provided this increased political capability does not detract from his own or from that of his interest groups, in which case he may resist.

Thus it can thus be seen that the member of an organization can be subjected to loyalty conflicts regarding himself, his interest groups, and his organization.

*   For instance, a business school professor found himself in each of these types of situations in the course of a single negotiation. He was chosen by the school to negotiate and design a course for middle managers of a prestigious company that wanted a long-term management-training program designed specifically for their industry. At that point, the school was undergoing rapid expansion and teaching resources were severely strained. At the same time, he was a member of a coalition of professors in the school who were determined to upgrade the quantity and quality of research done by the school. The professor was asked to negotiate a low price in order to ensure that the company could be locked in to the business school rather than let a rival business school secure the contract. This he strongly resisted, arguing that to do so would increase the load on the existing staff who were already overloaded because it would not generate the funds flow that would make it possible to take on additional staff. The school eventually agreed to setting a much higher price than originally envisioned. Thus, if it won the contract, it would have the funds to employ extra staff members for teaching; while,

if it lost the contract, the coalition would at least not have an additional teaching load. However, when it came to designing the course, a conflict arose between the coalition supporting the research focus and the professor himself. The coalition wanted to structure courses in such a way that a minimum of teaching was done and attention could be directed to research. The professor felt that, if the contract did succeed, his personal reputation as the designer of the course was at stake and would not be enhanced in industry by the design of a course with low exposure to the instructors. Therefore, he strongly resisted the coalition's demands and argued for a course design that would have a substantial instructor/student interaction content in the first cycle of the program. So, while he supported the coalition in resisting the organization's decision to go for the contract at low price, he resisted the coalition's decision to reduce the teaching content of the program.

In the preceding discussion, we have seen that one of the frequent options available to the political actor is to join coalitions. This will now receive further attention.

COALITIONS AND INTEREST GROUPS

THE EVOLUTION OF COALITIONS

The individual in an organization seldom has the necessary power and influence to dictate to his organization. If he wishes the organization to carry out actions that he desires, his power and influence must somehow be enhanced. We have pointed out that one of the bases of power is control of alternatives. The reason why coalitions form is that, by doing so, they reduce the alternatives available to the organization.

- In an extreme case, the firm has great power with respect to the individual worker and can play one worker off against the other, but if all workers unite to form a coalition (called a union in this case), the alternatives available to the organization are reduced back to one monolithic, and thus powerful, unit.

- In the same way, the chief executive may be able to coerce his senior managers individually; but, if they form a coalition stating that they will all resign if the firm does not expand its facilities instead of diversifying (as happened in the example described in chapter 2), the chief executive's power against this collective demand by his managers is reduced considerably.

However, coalition formation has its own problems, as we have seen already, in that coalition members do not join the coalition without bringing with them their demands, and the support of these coalition members could easily be given to alternative coalitions. In effect, then, a coalition is a small-scale suborganization in the broader environment, which is the actual organization. Each coalition must defend itself from competition for its members from other coalitions. Hence members of the group will be able to make demands on the coalition. These demands are related to the individual member's goals and form two broad classes.

1.   Demands on the coalition to satisfy the *current* wants and needs of the individual.

2.   Demands that are related to the individual's desire to ensure the future satisfaction of his needs and wants.

This second set of demands is of interest. Each member of the coalition would like to see the coalition set certain goals for itself, because the achievement of these goals would promote the individual goals of each coalition member.

- For instance, the draftsman in the earlier example demanded that the coalition set a goal of increasing staff, rather than increasing pay, before he would provide support. Increasing staff would cause a reduction in overtime, which fitted in with his personal goals.

- A group of newspaper reporters were trying to get one of the more influential reporters to join them in their attempts to get more pages in the newspaper issues. She would not provide this support unless they agreed to demand that at least some of the extra pages be devoted to articles and reports of interest to working women, since she felt strongly that the paper was underrepresenting this area, in which she was very strongly interested.

Each member of a coalition will, therefore, make a set of demands on the coalition to *commit itself to certain goals*. To obtain and/or retain the support of its members, the coalition as a whole must try to satisfy these demands by making commitments to pursue these goals. However, it is often impossible for the coalition to satisfy *all* of the demands of *all* of its coalition members, since, by nature, individuals are so varied that their goals can never be perfectly congruent. To overcome this problem, the coalition as a whole can develop a set of commitments with regard to *generalized* goals. These are goals that are phrased in *general*, rather than *specific*, terms. Because they are not too specific, they ensure the support of more members (who see *scope* for their own goal achievement). These commitments to strive for generalized goals are defined as *policy commitments*.

- Consider the case of the group of reporters in the preceding example. While all of the reporters were seeking to have the size of the paper increased, there were several subgroups, each of which had its own ideas as to who would get the increase. If the commitments of the group leaders had been phrased in specific terms, stating that they would press for X pages of extra sports coverage and Y pages of political coverage, they would have lost the support of the woman reporter. Instead, they committed themselves to pressing for a general increase in the size of the paper, in which space for sports, politics, women's interests, and several other topics would be decided later. In this way, they retained the support of many more coalition members than they would have had if they had been specific. The main point was to get the concession from management; then it would be possible for each member to start jockeying for space for their particular interests.

In summary, coalition members make demands on the coalition to strive for certain goals, and the coalition as a whole makes policy commitments in response to these demands. The coalition members then must decide whether these policy commitments are acceptable enough to warrant supporting the coalition.

A potential member of a political coalition will, therefore, join that coalition and contribute his resources *only* if he feels that the policy commitments of the coalition will promote his own goals. He will be content to stay with the political coalition as long as the performance of the coalition appears to be realizing these policies and is successful, or he will stay as long as he *expects* it to be successful (in the future.) If his requirements are not met, he may seek membership in an alternative coalition.

Members that the coalition gains must be protected from competing coalitions. As with the individual, the coalition can resort to manipulation or accommodation to achieve this end. Like the individual, the coalition can accommodate by bargaining with other coalitions or by forming supercoalitions with other coalitions.

With his background, it is now possible to start discussing the formation of multiple-person coalitions.

FORMATION OF
MULTIPLE–PERSON COALITIONS

Instead of proceeding from an existing coalition, assume that there are numerous individuals who have not yet formed coalitions. It is virtually impossible for an individual to achieve all his goals using only his own resources—he is dependent upon the cooperation of other individuals to achieve many of them. If all the actors in a situation had *completely* similar goals, coalition formation would present no problems. The coalition would consist of all the actors. All that would have to be decided would be the final allocation of the rewards gained from the coalition's activities. This would be accomplished by a multi-person bargaining process. However, in the more realistic case, where the goals of actors are inconsistent, competitive coalitions arise. Hence, despite the fact that a group of actors may have a large number of common goals, the formation of a grand coalition of all the actors is prevented by actors who have perhaps a few conflicting goals and so make conflicting demands. Two demands that are in conflict become an *issue* in a potential coalition situation. *Coalitions form when groups of individuals start taking sides on such issues.*

As the number of individuals in a situation increases, the number of individual goals that have to be satisfied in any potential coalition increases accordingly. It becomes increasingly difficult for any potential coalition to satisfy all these goals simultaneously or even to promise to satisfy them all. In any given situation, a number of possible coalitions could form.

- Cyert and March (1964) give the hypothetical example of a nine-person committee that had to decide on a painting for a village hall. (This is somewhat modified below.)

The nine members individually make the following demands.

A.   The painting must be an abstract monotone.

B.   The painting must be an impressionistic oil.

C.   The painting must be small and oval in shape.

D.   The painting must be small and in oil.

E.   The painting must be square in shape and multicolored.

F.   The painting must be impressionistic and square in shape.

G.   The painting must be a monotone and in oils.

H.   The painting must be multicolored and impressionistic.

I.   The painting must be small and oval in shape.

Here, each potential coalition member makes two simple demands regarding the color, shape, style, size, or medium of the painting. Assuming that only five members are required to make the decision (that is, a majority vote), there are three feasible coalitions: A, C, D, G, and I can form a coalition and commission a small, oval, monotone, abstract oil; B, C, D, H, and I can form a coalition and commission a small, oval, multicolored, impressionistic oil; B, D, E, F, and H can form a coalition and commission a small, square, multicolored, impressionistic oil. (Note that committee member D is needed in every possible coalition.)

Since the support of member D is essential to any successful coalition, the demands of D have to be met, and we can be sure that the final painting, if nothing else, will be small and in oil!

The *priority* with which issues are considered may have a significant effect on the way in which coalitions are formed.

- For instance, if the color issue (monotone versus multicolored) is given first priority and the style (abstract versus impressionistic) second priority, then two definite coalitions could form immediately: A-C-G-I and B-E-F-H, both competing for D's support. If, however, the style issue has first priority, followed by the shape issue, then three coalitions of two members each would form: A-G, B-H, and E-F. Then A-G would compete with B-H for the support of C, I ,and D, and E-F would seek the support of B-H and D. If B-H does not succeed in gaining the support of I and C, then the situation will revert to A-C-G-I and B-E-F-H competing for support of D. If B-H does succeed, then the resulting coalitions will be B-C-H-I, A-G-E-F, and D. In this case, A-G and E-F could form a *blocking* coalition, A-G-E-F, with the sole purpose of persuading D *not* to join the other coalition, which wants to commission a small, oval, multicolored, impressionistic oil. A-G and E-F have no *positive* interest in coalescing, their goals are incompatible.

The *priority* given to issues could, therefore, be an important determinant of the formation of coalitions. Out of the above discussion, three points of implication for political strategy formulation arise. First, the formation of coalitions is a function of the issues that potential members of the coalition perceive in the situation. Second, the formation of coalitions is a function of the priority that is attached to each issue. Third, it is not inconceivable that an uneasy alliance of enemies can join together with the express purpose of stopping a decision from taking place via a *blocking* coalition.

These factors provide an important means of *controlling* coalition formation in a political strategy move; for, if the political strategist makes astute use of these factors, he can do much to ensure that some issues are more visible to the players than others; and he may be able to exercise some control on the order in which these issues are discussed.

- Think back on any of the recent presidential campaigns and consider the extent to which the candidates attempted to raise issues before the nation and to attract public attention to issues that suited them, rather than their opponents. Consider how public opinion shifted as a candidate pushed favorable issues for himself into the public eye and forced the less successful opponent to defend himself against these issues.

- The marketing manager of an insurance company was on the brink of launching a large product development campaign. At the next management meeting, it had been decided to discuss poor profit performance in the previous two quarters. At issue was whether to deploy resources to expanding sales or to cutting costs by increasing automation (via electronic data processing). He knew that if this issue were to be raised at the meeting, he would be outvoted by a small majority of peers who leaned toward investing the funds in automation. However, he was convinced that automation didn't sell insurance! Therefore, he needed to find an issue that would rearrange the coalition structure currently against him. He realized that the key issue that he would prefer to have discussed was market share and not profits, so he did three things. First, he sent a report to all the management committee members that showed how losses in market share could be regained by his proposal. Second, he sent to all members of the management committee a memo asking them to consider ways in which his proposed product development program could be carried out effectively and at a lower cost. Third, he persuaded the chief executive to place his project proposal first on the agenda. When the meeting started, the issue was not whether the product launch should take place or not, but what funds would be required to launch the product; the automation proposal was postponed, because some marginal members of the automation coalition had become committed to the marketshare issue.

Another important facet of coalition formation needs to be discussed. Coalitions are formed in the first place because the organization does not have the resources to provide for the complete satisfaction of all the members' goals. Therefore, people join coalitions to try to persuade the organization to pursue directions that suit their goals. Now, obviously, if everyone were in the coalition, we would be back where we started. Riker (1962), in his analysis of political coalitions, argued that coalitions strive to reach the smallest size required for the coalition to get their way. Although there is some uncertainty about what the smallest size is that stops the coalition from *reaching* the smallest size, it seems logical to try to structure the coalition as small as is possible for the coalition to succeed, since the "spoils" that have to be divided up between the winners are then greater.

- If we consider the reporters' coalition discussed earlier, this applies. The more people the reporters get in their coalition, the fewer pages left per coalition member once these extra pages have been extracted from the management.

In the formation of a political strategy, the judgment as to what the size of the winning coalition should be is an important consideration in choosing the potential members. Yet another important (but risky) aspect of the Riker's size principle is the *timing*. If individuals are prepared to wait it out before committing themselves to an issue and joining one or another coalition, then the marginal value of their support becomes larger, the closer the coalition comes to the minimum size and the more the coalition will be prepared to offer them in concession if they join the coalition.

- Suppose committee member D held out in the example from Cyert and March. He could have three coalitions begging him to cast his vote in their favor and could extract concessions from them far in excess of what he could get if he committed himself early in the process.

- We see this phenomenon occur in many multiparty governments in which there are two major groups that do not have enough votes for a clear majority without the support of a small party (such as the British Liberal party). On occasions such as this, the Liberal party can extract major policy commitments from the Conservative party or the Labor party before it consents to support that party in the parliamentary voting.

However, a fencesitting tactic is not without risk; for, once the coalition has drawn in enough supporters to get its way, those who are not in the coalition are no longer necessary and will only decrease the payment to existing members if they are included. Therefore, if individuals wait too long, they may find themselves locked out of the winning coalition.

If we go back to the Cyert and March example above, two further points come up: the problems of the complexity of multiple issues and the problems of communications.

Problems of the Complexity of Multiple Issues

The Cyert and March example was deliberately simple. The issues in the example are clear-cut and dichotomous. In more complex political situations, the issues are more complex and less concrete and often are more concerned with the *degree* of goal attainment. The implementation of the policy commitments regarding these issues can be an extremely lengthy process (for instance, the creation of law and order in a big city). Also, not all issues can be resolved simultaneously; the coalition, having limited resources, must pay attention to more urgent issues and postpone less urgent ones until resources are available. Now, how does the coalition determine which issues are urgent? Urgency is, to some extent, determined by the intensity of the coalition members' demands for attention to the issue.

Problems of Communications

Obviously, a large amount of interaction must take place between all the committee members in Cyert and March's example before the issues can be decided. In more complex situations, where large numbers of people are involved, obviously, it is impossible for them all to bargain simultaneously with each other regarding the issues involved, but somehow these issues must be resolved! A situation like this results in the evolution of a more sophisticated political structure in an organization. By a process of differentiation, certain actors in the situation assume specific political roles and a hierarchical structure develops.

The next chapter will be devoted to how such a political structure develops in an organization.

SUMMARY: KEY CONCEPTS

1. Certain individuals can behave as political actors in an organization by striving to restructure conditions such that the organization pursues goals that suit these actors.

2. These actors tends to use manipulation, bargaining, and coalition formation with interest groups to achieve their purposes.

3. Coalitions, in order to retain the support of their members, make policy commitments to generalized goals, so that individual members see some possibility of achieving their own goals.

4. Coalitions tend to build around issues.

5. Some control of coalition structure may be achieved by making different issues visible.

6. Coalitions attempt to reach the smallest size possible in order to have their way. This increases the per-capita rewards for the successful coalition.

7. Fence sitters may be able to extract larger rewards by holding back their support of the coalition, but they run the risk of being shut out once the coalition has reached the size necessary to achieve success.

5

The Evolution
of Political Structures
in Organizations

In this chapter, our deliberate political perspective will be focused on the internal processes operating in organizations. An understanding of the political content of organizational behavior is essential for the formulation of political strategies. First, the chapter will explain the relationships between an organization and its environment, and it will identify the major types of relationships that exist. It then will develop a conceptual understanding of the way in which an organization maintains its environmental support. Out of this will flow an analysis of how the organization facing complexity will go about handling that complexity. From this, the development of coalitions and interest groups within organizations will be traced, and the evolution of a political structure in an organization will be analyzed. Finally, the impact of coalition and interest group behavior on the policy formulation and execution processes will be developed.

The arguments in this chapter are drawn primarily from the conceptual work of Cyert and March (1964), Katz and Kahn (1966), March and Simon (1967), and Thompson (1967). Once again, interested readers are encouraged to pursue their specific interests by referring to these works.

ORGANIZATIONS AS SYSTEMS:
A CHANGE IN PERSPECTIVE

So far, this text has focused on the behavior of an individual actor, and that actor could be either a person, a group, a firm, or even a nation. Now, for a while, it is appropriate to shift focus to an organization.

In all but the most primitive circumstances, actors in a society are dependent upon other actors for their survival. Very few individuals are self-sufficient enough to be able to provide all the input that they require for physical and emotional health. In the same way, no firm or other type of organization has complete command of all the resources necessary for its well-being.

Thus, all organizations are dependent upon the environment for the provision of certain inputs; which the organization then transforms into outputs; which it, in turn, uses to get more inputs. Organizational environmental relations thus tend to show a general pattern of exchange/transformation/exchange.

The first part of this discussion focuses on some of the characteristics of this input-dependence problem facing all organizations. Let us look at the problem of input dependency from the point of view of, say, a manufacturing firm. If this firm is to survive, it must obtain inputs from the environment. Raw materials are needed to manufacture the product. Labor and management are needed to process raw materials. Funds are needed to buy equipment. At the other end, customers are needed to buy the products, and funds are needed to pay the employees. So a cyclical pattern of input exchange to transformation to output exchange is followed; and, if this does not take place, the organization cannot survive.

However, the inputs that are provided are generally scarce. Raw materials, labor, funds, and customers are not unlimited, and there are other organizations in the environment that compete for those inputs. Chamberlain (1955) points out that the competitive nature of the environment gives rise to two major types of relationships between the organization and elements of the environment. These are symbiotic relations and commensal relations.

SYMBIOTIC AND
COMMENSAL RELATIONS

Symbionts are those elements of the environment on which the organization is dependent for inputs. These are not confined to the current providers of input but also include the potential providers of input. The type of relationship that exists between the organization and its symbionts is a special one that strongly influences their behavior with respect to one another, since the organization depends for its very survival upon its symbionts. Without them, it would not get the inputs it needs to survive. The symbionts in turn depend upon the organization to take their outputs; so, without the organization *or others like it*, the symbionts could not survive. Hence, the relationship between the symbionts and the organization is one in which all must cooperate even though they are in conflict as to how to cooperate. This theme of conflict over cooperation captures the essence of the way in which symbiont organizations behave with respect to one another.

- For instance, a manufacturing firm must have customers. If it is providing a desirable product, the customers want the product. Hence, to meet their wants, customer and firm *must* cooperate in exchanging product for payment. The conflict that arises is over the *price* of the exchange. The firm might try other customers and the customers might try other firms, but, if both are to have their needs satisfied, there must be some manufacturers and some customers. Symbionts cannot, or do not, want to do without one another.

Commensals, on the other hand, are those elements in the environment that are trying to attract the organization's symbionts. We use the term *commensals* instead of *competitors,* because we need a generic word that reflects the general nature of the relationship. A firm may be competing with other industries or with organizations such as banks or even the government in trying to secure certain inputs (such as computer programmers or funds for expansion).

The essence of the relationship between commensals is far more competitive than is the relationship between symbionts. They do not need one another to survive. Although it may be possible for them to cooperate at times, as we will see later, this type of cooperation is not essential. It is one of expedience that is often plagued by the danger of one of the "cooperating" commensal's cheating.

Having defined the terms *symbiont* and *commensal* and having identified the nature of the relationship between these and the organization, let us now consider how they interact in a competitive system.

INDUCEMENT–CONTRIBUTION EXCHANGES

The organization exchanges its outputs for its symbiont's inputs. To simplify the discussion, let the exchange be regarded as an exchange of an *inducement* to the symbiont (the organization's output) for a *contribution* by the symbiont (the organization's input).

- For instance, an employer may exchange a salary (inducement) *out*put for an employee's labor (contribution) *in*put. Alternatively, a retailer may exchange a product (inducement) *out*put for a customer's money (contribution) *in*put.

This inducement-contribution agreement between the two parties must be acceptable *to both.*

The *organization* decides whether the contribution it is receiving is sufficient for the inducement it is offering. This, in part, is determined by the inducement/contribution offers it can receive from *alternative* symbionts.

On the other hand, the *symbiont* decides whether the inducement it is being offered is sufficient for the contribution it is required to make. This, too, is determined partly by the *alternative* inducement/contribution offers it can receive from the commensals of the organization. The symbiont attempts to make the minimum contribution for a given inducement.

Unless *both* the organization and the symbiont are of the opinion that such an agreement will be *beneficial* and *inexpensive* to both parties, relative to the alternatives available, agreement will not be reached.

Under conditions of scarcity of resources, the symbionts attempt to obtain as high an inducement as possible and simultaneously attempt to give as low a contribution as possible in exchange.

Before actually *giving* their support, the symbionts make inducement demands on the organization. If unchecked, the *aspired* demands of the symbionts exceed the organization's capacity to fulfill them; so, it must find some means of limiting these demands. One of the strategies the organization can employ is to use its resources to restructure the situation in such a way that the domain symbionts are induced, coerced, persuaded, or obligated to provide the support. Alternatively, by using the resources at its disposal, the organization can block the access of its symbionts to its commensals or block access of commensals to domain symbionts.

However, the organization seldom reaches a political position that permits it unilaterally to dictate action in its entire environment. There are so many symbionts and commensals that the limits of the organization's political capability will be reached long before it has subjugated every symbiont and every commensal.

In chapter 6, some of the alternative political actions available to the organization will be discussed. Here, however, we wish to explore the problem that faces the organization when it tries to cater to the many demands made on it by its various symbionts. Because of the limits on its own political capability, the usual organization is faced with the problem of handling multiple demands.

MULTIPLE DEMANDS ON ORGANIZATIONS

- During the "stagflation" period of the United States economy in the early to the middle seventies, a manufacturer faced the following problems. His bank was calling for him to improve his liquidity, customers were demanding lower prices, his suppliers were asking for earlier payment on his raw materials, his workers were demanding increases in wages, and the shareholders were getting very vociferous about profit improvement and a better dividend payment. The interesting thing about the demands that this manufacturer faced was that not only did the demands far exceed his capacity to meet them, but, when you think about it, many of the demands were conflicting. To improve liquidity for the banks requires funds, but suppliers wanted these funds to pay for materials. To improve profits required cuts in costs or increases in prices, but labor wanted to raise costs and customers wanted to reduce prices. To increase dividends decreased cash and this affected liquidity.

Although this example is drawn from a time when the economy was undergoing exceptional turmoil, it is not unusual in these times of rapid change for organizations to face pressures from their symbionts that exceed their capacities to meet them. It is also not unusual for them to manifest conflicts and inconsistencies within themselves. The larger the organization, the more complex these demands become, and very soon the capacity of a single manager in the organization to cope with this complexity is completely overwhelmed.

The organization's response to this is to differentiate its structure—to form subparts in the organization that specialize in handling specific relationships with the symbionts in the environment.

- So, for instance, a purchasing department will be created to handle raw materials, a personnel department to handle human resources, a financial department to handle funds flow, a products department to handle physical productions, and so on. Not only does this give rise to more efficiency, because specialists are given narrower, more comprehensible tasks to do well instead of trying to do everything superficially, it also creates conditions that stop the organization from becoming totally paralyzed by the complexity and uncertainty it faces.

- For example, we can say to the sales manager that he is in charge of sales; and, given the direction to go out and sell, he can go out and really push sales without worrying (too much) about whether the raw materials, labor, and products will be there when delivery time comes. At the same time, the manufacturing manager can plan the production of products without having to worry about whether they will be sold or whether the labor and materials will be there. The specialized parts of the organization serve the function of absorbing some of the uncertainty for the other parts. At the same time, these parts are insulated from the demands being placed on other parts.

So, because it is virtually impossible to make rational decisions in the face of conflicting demands, what the organization does is place a boundary around each aspect of the problem (for example, sales) and give a person within that boundary the means to make a rational decision without having to worry about the conflicting demands and high level of uncertainty that the organization as a whole faces. However, the very fact that a set of specialized departments is introduced into the organization creates new problems. For the people in charge of these functions develop a narrower, more specialized *perspective*. The sales manager starts to seek sales, and he sees everything from a sales point of view, including the production department that appears to be continually complaining about schedule disruptions. The production manager becomes obsessed with the efficiency of production and sees the sales department as an endless *source* of schedule disruptions.

Thus, out of specialization (or differentiation) arise multiple goals within the organization, which tend to be aligned to the multiple demands flowing in from the symbionts. Couple this with the fact that the individuals in charge of divisions, departments, and so on each bring to the organization their own sets of aspirations and goals, and we have a situation that is rife with potential goal conflicts.

In this text, the subject of goals will be treated with the deliberate political perspective with which we started. The text by Max Richards, *Organizational Goal Structures* will consider goals from other perspectives, and it is a great deal more detailed.

The problem that the differentiated or specialized organization faces is that the narrower perspective created by the departmentalization gives rise to interest groups and coalitions within the departments. Individuals, in pursuit of their own goals and within their narrower perspective, tend to seek others who would like the same goals achieved.

And so, the coalition formation process that was discussed in chapter 4, coupled with the problems of complexity and communication that we discussed in the closing of chapter 4, emerges. We saw that, in a large organization, it is impossible for all members of the organization to communicate with all others in this multiple-person situation, and some means of resolving this problem has to be developed. As we will see below, this problem gives rise to a political structure in the organization.

POLITICAL STRUCTURES WITHIN ORGANIZATIONS

EMERGENCE OF FIDUCIARY ROLES

It is impossible for all the members of a large organization to communicate with all the other members. What basically happens in large organizations is that members of coalitions tend to allocate to one of their number a "fiduciary" role—a role in which the authority to make decisions for the coalition as a whole is vested in one person, who then acts as a representative of the group's interests in communications with other groups. This person may or may not be a manager of the group members. If the subordinates feel that the manager is not representing their interests well enough, they may elect a fiduciary among themselves to represent them against the manager or to represent them over the head of their manager.

Thus, a fiduciary is a political actor who represents an underlying coalition. His role is to use the resources placed at his disposal to manipulate or to accommodate other fiduciaries. In the process of representing his interest group, he may form supercoalitions with other fiduciaries, pooling resources with them. Depending upon the political capabilities of the participating fiduciaries, the rewards reaped by these supercoalitions will be allocated to the respective underlying coalitions that make up the supercoalitions. Since the effecting of such rewards also involves a time lag, the fiduciaries also demand policy commitments on the issues that are of interest to the underlying groups.

Since the interests of all coalitions are not identical, the fiduciary chooses to bargain only with those fiduciaries whose policy demands are not mutually exclusive to his. He will compete with the others.

In large organizations, supercoalitions bargain or compete with other supercoalitions, thus forming ever-larger coalitions in which fewer and fewer fiduciaries interact, each one representing the interests of larger and larger numbers of coalitions and their underlying beneficiaries. Eventually, the whole system of individuals will be characterized by a hierarchy of coalitions that culminates in a few major coalitions with some directly opposing interests. When we recall the way in which organizations develop specialized subsystems to cater with complexity, it is not surprising that these subsystems, with their narrower perspectives and rather specialized goals, often form the major coalitions.

● Thus, in any organization, we might find the marketing people and the production people who have their interests represented by a few powerful and influential representatives from the respective departments. Depending on the *relative* power and influence of these major departments, the one or the other might be able to have its way on the issues that are being faced in the organization.

As these large and complex coalitions start to form, the nature of the fiduciary role becomes more complex, and we see a new role emerging—that of the political leader.

A *political leader* is a political actor who is the fiduciary of a major coalition. At this level of the hierarchy, such a person has to comply with certain special requirements, the most important of which is the ability to accept a complex mass of policy demands and to create a suitable set of policy commitments that will satisfy his underlying coalitions and also prove operationally adequate to ensure that the organization survives. The set of leaders form an inner circle that determines the political direction for the organization as a whole.

Since the leaders of the major coalitions cannot hope to satisfy all the demands simultaneously, they evolve a set of *general policy commitments* that aims to satisfy the majority of the demands represented in the groups. This policy formation process will be discussed next.

THE POLICY FORMATION PROCESS

The process of policy formation can be seen in the terms presented in Figure 5.1.

First, look at the bottom left-hand side of Figure 5.1. The external members, after due consideration of their alternatives, make demands on external fiduciaries. The external fiduciaries transmit these demands to the political leaders of the organization (who are responsible for policy formulation).

Simultaneously, internal members (see the bottom right-hand corner of Figure 5.1) make demands on internal fiduciaries, who transmit these as both policy demands and inducement demands to the leaders of the organization.

Figure 5.1.　Policy Formulation Process.

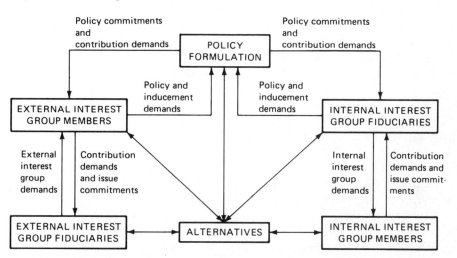

Source: "Organization Dynamics: MBL (General Management) Cycle III, Guide 3," University of South Africa, 1975. Reprinted by permission.

The leaders of the organization receive these two sets of demands. On the basis of the alternatives available to them, they begin manipulating and accommodating the external and internal fiduciaries in order to determine the terms on which these inducement demands are to be met. The leaders of the organization manipulate the situation to ensure that the terms of exchange favor the organization as far as possible. They bargain with fiduciaries by countering their policy and inducement demands with policy commitments and contribution demands.

- For illustrative purposes, let us look at the case of a travel company and some of the demands that it faced over a six-month period.

External Groups

The company chartered space on vessels for sea cruises. Its major supplier, besides the *inducement demands* relating to charter prices, demanded the following *policy commitments*: that the company enter into a three-year contract guaranteeing a certain minimum volume of passengers to each destination; that the company demand from all passengers who booked on a tour a 25-percent deposit that would immediately be forwarded to the shipping company.

Banks: The company's major bank required that the company commit itself to creating an account in which all customers' prepayments be deposited to offset the current overdraft and that the overdraft at no stage exceed a certain level of dollars or a certain multiple of the prepayments account.

Agents: The company's five major agents, who sold about 40 percent of its volume, demanded that the company institute a policy of setting aside a guaranteed proportion of berths for each of them for each tour that were to be released to other agents only after the agents had had some time to sell these berths.

Internal Groups

Branch Offices: A spokesperson for the branch office managers demanded that the branches be paid the same commission as outside agents. At the time, they received a smaller commission.

Tour Leaders: Each tour had a leader who represented the company and handled passenger problems. A spokesperson from the tour leaders demanded a "discomfort allowance" for any of the leaders who spent more than a certain number of days per quarter away from home. To date, all employees had been on straight salaries. This was the first demand for a differentiated salary structure.

Marketing Department: Traditionally, the company had spent most of its promotion funds by marketing in the printed media. The marketing department demanded that the company change to use of visual and audio media, with a substantial increase in budget.

Policy Decisions

After viewing the alternatives available to the company and the relative political capabilities of the opponents in each case, the company formulated the following policy decisions.

Suppliers: The supplier was an important component in the company's overall strategy and some concessions were made. The company committed itself to the following policy decisions: that the company would guarantee, via a three-year contract, a minimum volume of dollar business but *not* by destination; and that the company would retain all monies paid in advance by customers, because this was in fact trust money.

Bank: That the company would maintain overdraft levels below a certain level of dollars specified by month to take into account cyclicality of sales. Eventually, the company changed banks.

Agents: That all agents would have equal access to berth availability, unless agents were prepared to guarantee sales.

Bank Managers: That branch offices would receive the same commission as agents but that they then would pay to the head office a service charge for all expenses incurred by the head office on behalf of branches, plus a financial fee for head office overheads.

Tour Leaders: That no tour leader would spend more than a certain number of days per quarter away from home without receiving compensating vacation in another quarter.

Marketing Department: That the promotion budget would remain unchanged but would be used at the discretion of the marketing department.

In the process of policy formation that has been described, two facets of the demands of particular interest to the political strategist are worth considering in more detail.

Irrefutable Demands and Conflicting Demands

Particularly powerful or influential groups inside or outside the organization can make demands that *have* to be met if their valuable support is to be maintained. These irrefutable demands constitute the *primary constraints* on the organization.

There may be times when demands on the organization are in conflict, yet the groups making these conflicting demands are sufficiently powerful for the organization to have to try to satisfy them. There are two basic strategies that can be employed in handling such demands.

Compromise: An attempt can be made to negotiate a compromise between the conflicting groups.

Generalize: We have already argued above that, when the policy commitments are made sufficiently general, both groups can see some scope for achieving their specific purposes.

- A company manufacturing electronic instruments was facing decreasing profit margins due to rapidly escalating costs in a tight market. The shareholders were pressing for increased profits; and the workers were becoming increasingly concerned about layoffs, and they were threatening to unionize if major layoffs took place. Senior management formulated a policy designed to appease demands for more profits and work force stability by formulating a policy of "increased profitability and growth through more productive use of existing resources." This was interpreted by shareholders as a commitment to improving profitability and by the work force as a commitment to maintaining stability of employment. Because the commitment had been phrased in a general way it obviated specific demands from shareholders to cut costs, notably labor costs, and it obviated specific demands from the work force to guarantee job security.

Thus, generalization of policy commitments is a useful tool for handling conflicting demands from powerful coalitions. There is, however, a third technique that can be employed in the face of this dilemma—*sequential attention.*

Pay Sequential Attention.

If an organization faces a number of demands that are inconsistent with one another, it may be possible to handle this conflict by focusing on one demand at a time while at the same time holding the others in check.

• Consider the case of a production vice-president who was facing demands from customers for better service and quality improvement, demands from his department for increased salaries, and demands from the senior vice-president for reducing escalating costs. What the vice-president did was to try to hold quality and delivery at current levels while he improved productivity in the manufacturing plants. He used some of the improvements in productivity to inch up the salaries and wages. As the demands from the customers became more insistent, he switched attention from cost reduction and salary improvement and tried to keep them at satisfactory levels while he made improvements in quality and delivery in order to mollify the customers. As the customers started to quiet down, he turned his attention to the cost problem in earnest, since by now management was getting impatient with the fact that costs were still not declining. Having demonstrated some decline in costs, he could then press for wage and salary improvements in response to the department's complaints that these had been stalled for some time. In this way, he was able to balance a stream of conflicting demands that were, essentially, inconsistent with one another.

Sequential attention to commitments or demands involves paying attention to the demonstration of improvement on one set of demands, while holding the other demands at a level that at least keeps the demanders satisfied, and then changing attention from the demand on which improvement has been demonstrated to one on which the demands are becoming increasingly insistent. Then, the cycle is repeated all over again. It is the only tool that one can resort to when one faces conflicting demands that cannot be compromised, if one cannot formulate a policy commitment that is general enough for all parties to see some scope for the achievement of their purposes.

This concludes our discussion of the process of policy formulation. We now will give some attention to policy execution.

THE POLICY INTERPRETATION
AND EXECUTION PROCESS

Once the policy decisions flowing from the policy formulation process have been accepted by coalitions in the organization, policy execution must take place. It must be remembered that the organization must convert inputs from the environment into inducement outputs. This transformation of inputs into outputs must, however, be guided, monitored, and controlled to ensure that the transformations and transactions take place in terms of the formulated policy. The actual detailed and specific sets of small actions that must be carried out to effect this transformation are *technical* actions, which occur at the technical level of the organization (say the shop floor).

Policy decisions are phrased in broad terms, since they are formulated as *general* guides to action. Thus, they cannot be applied to specific circumstances without interpretation. Therefore, some system of action between the policy formulation level and the technical level is necessary. The functions of this intermediary system are to receive policy-decision signals; to interpret these signals for specific situations that arise; in terms of its interpretation of policy, to create specific tasks for the execution of the policies by the technical level; to monitor the performance of the technical level and to adjust action at the level at which action departs from policy; and to mobilize the resources necessary to effect these technical tasks. Parsons (1969) calls these functions of organization the administrative functions. To enable such functions to be executed, an intermediate level is required in the organization. The primary function of this level is the interpretation and execution of policy. The organization evolves a hierarchy of administrative offices to perform this task.

The tasks of the incumbents of these offices can be divided into two categories: mediation between the organization and the outside to obtain the resources needed to execute policy; and administration of the organization's internal affairs to ensure that policy is executed. The flow of interaction between the three organizational levels, and between the levels and their environment, is diagrammed in Figure 5.2.

At the administrative level, managers face a variety of inducement demands from both external and internal interest groups. The managers interpret the policy directives in terms of the specific demands made on them, and then they undertake a negotiating process to determine the terms on which inducements will be exchanged for contributions from the external and internal interest groups. When the terms have been agreed upon, the administrative level generates tasks for the technical level to perform in order to execute the policy. Task directives are transmitted to the technical level.

Figure 5.2. Policy Execution in a Political System.

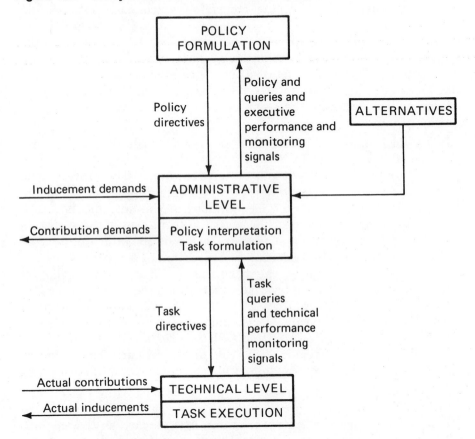

Source: "Organization Dynamics: MBL (General Management) Cycle III, Guide 3," University of South Africa, 1975. Reprinted by permission.

At the technical level, the actual contributions of the interest groups are received and converted, according to task directives, into actual inducements that are dispatched to interest groups.

The administrative level receives two forms of feedback from the technical level. First, task queries are transmitted to the administrative level when situations not covered by the task directives arise. Second, performance is monitored to ensure that the technical level is, in fact, operating as directed.

Similarly, the policy formulation level receives policy queries and managerial/performance feedback.

When we combine the policy formulation and policy execution processes of the organization, the full set of political processes of the organization can be illustrated as in Figure 5.3.

Figure 5.3. Total Flow of Political Action in an Organization.

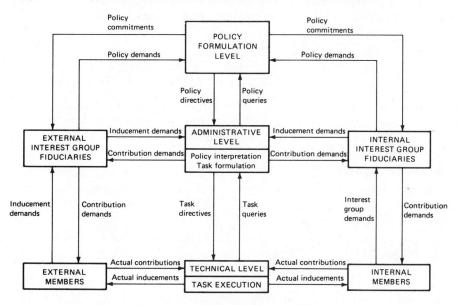

Source: "Organization Dynamics: MBL (General Management) Cycle III, Guide 3," University of South Africa, 1975. Reprinted by permission.

Since Figure 5.3 is essentially a combination of Figures 5.1 and 5.2, there is little point in repeating the discussion. Reference, how-ever, should be made to a significant departure from Figure 5.1, in which all the interest group's demands were indicated as flowing into policy formulation.

In Figure 5.3 the inducement demands are shown as flowing into the administrative level of the policy execution branch. A prepon-derantly large proportion of such demands actually flows into this level, specifically to the managers (who are, in effect, formally ap-pointed fiduciaries of the organization) responsible for the mediat-ing function.

This finally completes the model of political action in organiza-tions. The questions that remain to be answered are those concerned with the relevance of this model to the concepts of political strategy.

POLITICAL STRATEGY
IMPLICATIONS

THE RELEVANCE
OF POLITICAL ACTION

The political strategist cannot afford to ignore the political action in organizations in the formulation of political strategy for these major reasons.

First, political strategy is formulated in the context of the strategist's own organization, and internal considerations place constraints on what strategies the formulator is *allowed* to use.

Second, political strategy is formulated in the context of the target organizations; that is to say, the political processes that take place within opposing organizations influence which counterstrategies they will be likely to employ, and the astute strategist cannot ignore counterstrategies.

Third, political strategy is concerned with the forging of alliances with other organizations. This alliance is, in fact, a superorganization in which the same types of political processes as we have described here take place at an interorganizational level. Such an alliance would be very difficult to hold together without an intimate knowledge of the processes that shape and hold together such an alliance.

Each of these perspectives now will be discussed in more detail.

CONSTRAINTS ON STRATEGY
AS A RESULT OF
INTERNAL POLITICAL PROCESSES

- One of the major frustrations that President John F. Kennedy experienced in the Cuban Missile crisis was discovering that at the time of the crisis the Jupiter missiles in Turkey, which he had ordered to be removed some months before, were still in place. His direct order had not been executed for months, because interest groups found ways of delaying implementation.

- A major agricultural importer at one stage decided to implement a program whereby its producing lands would be turned over to nationals in the country of production. The decision to do this was announced at the head office as a formal policy decision, but it took years to implement because of the resistance by the local management at regional level.

- The soap manufacturer discussed in chapter 1 was forced to postpone plans to diversify into food production because of the resistance of a powerful group of managers who demanded expansion of the soap production operation.

All of these examples are manifestations of situations in which internal political processes delayed or prevented the execution of a major policy decision. It is as well to recognize the internal politics of an organization before selecting a course of action.

The question that frequently arises is whether political processes should or can be eradicated in a formal organization. The contention here is that political processes are spontaneous, natural, and necessary phenomena in the organization. It is via political processes that the demands from the environment and from the organization's members are articulated. The chief executive cannot respond to all the demands being placed upon the organization. A well-managed political process provides a filter for all but the most important demands, provided that the chief executive understands the nature of political action. In essence, the chief executive (or any manager on a smaller scale) can control and channel political activity to the benefit of the organization. To stamp out politics is to deny organizations the flexibility necessary to adapt to the internal and external pressures.

The key to control of organizational politics lies in developing an ability to analyze organizational action in a political context. The political strategist should be aware of the major coalitions within the organization and of the power and influence of both internal and external interest groups. A knowledge of where the power and influence lies, and where it will lie in the future, gives the strategist the opportunity to anticipate political action and take steps to control this via adjustments in the authority structure of the internal system.

The second key to control of organizational politics has already been discussed. To a large extent, coalitions tend to build around issues and by controlling which issues will be given emphasis and which priorities will be attached to these issues, the strategist can channel political activity in directions that he feels suit the organization's interests.

Finally, the chief executive needs to be aware of the tools available for controlling conflicting demands made upon him. The techniques of compromise, generalization of policy commitments, and sequential attention to these commitments or to demands provide ways of maintaining a balance between such inconsistent demands.

So, political strategy is constrained by internal factors, and it is well to think through the responses that might be expected from internal interest groups if a specific strategic move is being contemplated. In some moves, speed, or intense organizational commitment, is of the essence, and a well-formulated strategy can be destroyed by reluctant executives acting on behalf of unpersuaded interest groups.

POLITICAL ACTION IN OPPONENTS' ORGANIZATIONS

An understanding of political processes is also necessary when one is contemplating a move against an opponent. In the first place, a thorough knowledge of the opponents' structures of the dominant coalitions provides a means of anticipating the countermoves that can be expected. As has been argued before, the idea of a unilateral strategy in which no counterresponses are expected is absurd.

The subject of anticipating strategic responses will be elaborated in chapter 6, but the point here is that a knowledge of the political processes operating within organizations is necessary if effective strategic anticipation is to be accomplished.

Another important area that emerges from analysis of the opponents' political system is the determination of their policy commitments. We saw in chapter 2 that the commitment structure of the opponents plays a major role in determining their influence base. The more one knows of their commitments to internal and external interest groups, the more one can identify avenues of action that are precluded from them out of their obligation to keep their commitments to these groups.

- The example in chapter 2 of the ill-fated public commitment by a large travel company to beat the prices of its competitors is of relevance here. The smaller company aggressively used the commitment by cutting its prices in the larger company's key market areas and then suggested to potential customers that they take up the bigger company's offer.

- During a boom period, a construction company waited until one of its major competitors was overcommitted on several long-term contracts before moving into mining construction, an area that traditionally had been the major preserve of the overcommitted company. By promising and demonstrating capacity to deliver the contracts on time, it managed to secure a foothold in an area where it traditionally would have had to buy market share at high cost.

- A new bank opened in a certain regional banking system with the slogan "We give loans to those that other banks turn down." Instead of trying to match this slogan, the major regional banks started turning away even more of their loan applicants particularly the riskier ones who promptly went to the new bank. When the economy turned down, the regional banks assisted in the bailing out of the newcomer, which soon found itself in tremendous difficulties with failed loans. This did permanent damage to the image of the new bank.

Creative analysis of the implications of competitors' commitments and policy statements opens many avenues for aggressive political strategy, many of which are enhanced by the knowledge of the political processes that give rise to these commitments.

Finally, knowledge of the political processes taking place in one's competitors' system creates opportunities for controlling interorganizational relations. We have already seen that coalitions tend to form around issues within organizations; this tends to apply in coalitions between organizations as well. By making some issues more visible than others, one may be able to create coalition structures that work to the benefit of the company.

- Regulating agencies are traditionally impervious to companies' appeals to reason, immune to threats, and unavailable for negotiation. Being bureaucracies, they cannot make exceptions with impunity, and their scope and the complexity they face makes it very important that they go by the book. To make exceptions is to invite bureaucratic chaos, since the first concession opens a floodgate of demands for more. An import/export agent in a foreign country was experiencing great difficulty with the local customs department for importing certain goods, because these goods had been classified as high duty goods rather than low duty goods. The problem was that the items being imported were unusual enough to be ambiguously classifiable. Once the classification had been made to the agent's disadvantage, the issue became whether it was the correct classification or not and the customs people refused to change the classification. The importer was astute enough to recognize that the issue had to be changed. As long as the classification issue was receiving attention, he faced a formidable coalition of customs officials who were determined to abide by the original ruling. Fortunately his overseas supplier was a potential customer for a local product that the country was keen to export. Therefore, he appealed to the Department of Exports to assist him in developing an export market for the local product, via his potential supplier. His argument was that the supplier might be lost if *his* products could not be sold locally and that the current duty would make it uneconomical to sell them locally. The issue then became one of international barter, and it became an issue between the Department of Customs and the Department of Exports. The reclassification took place in forty-eight hours.

Thus, creative focusing of issues within the target organization can be a useful way of altering the situation in favor of the political strategist.

MacMillan Strategy Form:Pol.Concepts CTB—4

The final area in which political processes are of relevance is in recognizing their validity for interorganizational processes. This topic is the main topic of chapter 6.

SUMMARY: KEY CONCEPTS

1. Organizations in the act of creating specialized departments also create grounds for potential goal conflicts, since departments develop a narrow specialized perspective.

2. Many relations between the organization and its symbionts are characterized by conflict over how to cooperate.

3. Many relations between the organization and its commensals are characterized by noncooperation or cooperation with incentive to cheat.

4. Policy commitments must be formulated to satisfy the demands of powerful internal and external interest groups.

5. In the cases in which these policy demands by interest groups are in conflict, three forms of response are available: compromise, generalization of policy commitments, and sequential attention to commitments.

6. The astute leader of a complex organization should be able to cope with the conflicting sets of demands facing him and recognize that it is only via management of the organizational political processes that a viable, adaptable organization can be maintained. It is through the political processes that disparate, but important, environmental demands are articulated.

7. Understanding political processes in organizations assists the political strategist in (a) avoiding strategies that will not be accepted by his own organization; (b) anticipating responses that opponents may make to his strategies; (c) identifying the policies and commitments that limit the opponents' actions; and (d) controlling the interorganizational coalitions of alliances he may form.

6

Interorganizational Political Action

POLITICAL ACTION
AMONG ORGANIZATIONS

The purpose of this chapter is to explore some of the political relations among organizations. There are a number of ways of viewing
interorganizational action, but, once again, a deliberately political perspective will be taken.

Two major facets of interorganizational action will be discussed.
The first facet concerns the options available to the organization in
formulating political strategy. The second is concerned with attempting to anticipate the responses of the target organization of a political
move, for, unless the fact that target organizations are going to react
to strategic moves is taken into account, the realism of any strategy is
in serious doubt.

It is stressed that the political strategy is concerned with reinforc-
ing the economic strategy of the organization, that without a sound
and viable economic strategy the organization will not be able to retain environmental support over time. However, having decided on
an economic strategy, the organization has a number of political options in deciding how to enhance this strategy.

POLITICAL OPTIONS

First we shall discuss the nature of the political relations between the firm and its environment and show how the firm could try to create a central position for itself in the environment.

The argument will be based on the approach of Schumpeter (1942) and Marchal (1951). In chapter 2 it was stated that the political capability of the firm depended on its political resources, that is, its power and influence bases. To ensure future political capability the firm can therefore attempt to expand or consolidate these bases.

Ideally, a firm exchanging with a part of the environment would structure conditions in the environment in such a way that the part with which it is exchanging has *no* alternative in the situation (alternatively, that it is totally committed to the firm). Such a condition ensures that the terms of exchange are best for the firm. Firms should strive to create such conditions in their environment or, at least, near approximations to these conditions, since this gives them maximum power or influence in the situation. This is generally a temporary condition, since elements in the environment can undertake political action to develop countervailing power to resist this control.

The political action of the firm can therefore be regarded as action to create and exploit a series of temporary control conditions with regard to elements of the environment and, as these controls are eroded by the reaction of the elements, continuously to create new control conditions.

In this section the general options available to the firm for creating control conditions will be identified. There is a confusingly large number of ways in which the firm can undertake political action to create the control conditions it desires. To reduce the confusion, it is useful to classify these ways along four dichotomous "dimensions."

Whether to Act Toward Symbionts or Commensals

Action toward Symbionts

For example, a manufacturer might attempt to secure a long-term contract with a supplier, thus securing supplies and blocking off a competitor from these supplies.

Action toward Commensals

For example, a group of companies in an industry might form an employers' association for negotiating with unions, thus preventing the unions from playing one organization off against the others.

Whether to Take
Direct or Indirect Action

Direct Action

For example, a company may attempt to develop specific influence with key customers by co-opting members onto the board.

Indirect Action

For example, a company could take control of a critical raw material supplier and use this to control the behavior of its competitors.

Whether to Take
Manipulative or
Accommodative Action

It should be clear that both can be done—in fact, one may try to manipulate the situation to create the best conditions for accommodation. The point is that the "dimensions" are not mutually exclusive—a well-conceived political strategy can use *combinations* of political actions, such as simultaneously taking direct, accommodative action against symbionts *and* indirect, manipulative action against commensals. Here we are primarily concerned with the *types of options* available. One of the broad options, then, is whether to act *primarily* by manipulation or by accommodation. One can conceive of several ways of accommodating with an element of the environment.

By Joint Commitment

By jointly committing themselves to a course of action, the firm and its target symbionts or commensals come to agreements as to how they are going to behave in the future.

- For example, a company can enter into a contract with one or more of its customers. For the length of that contract the firm is assured of output and customers are assured of input. Alternatively a company can enter into a joint agreement with its competitors regarding how they are going to handle unions or government agencies.

By Co-optation

By co-opting a powerful or influential member of the target organization into its policy making processes, the firm confers on the target element a certain amount of authority but at the same time hopes that the member will also consider the interests of the firm when he is participating in the policy formulation processes of the target organization.

- For instance, it is not uncommon to find the board of directors co-opting members who represent major creditors, such as banks.

By Coalescence

By coalescing, the organization and its target formally combine and pool their political resources against the environment. They both submit to the authority of the joint organization thus formed.

- For example, a merger between two competitors or a merger between a firm and a major supplier or customer combine the two organizations' financial, physical, and human reserves and equip them both with more political capability in their environment than if they continued to act as separate organizations. However, the coalescence need not be permanent. It is not uncommon in situations where the individual organizations do not have the resources to meet the challenges in the environment for one or more competitors to form a consortium. Their resources are pooled, and both companies give up their authority to a higher-order structure that persists until the challenge has been met and then disbands. This occurs frequently in the case of large projects, such as construction or military projects, where several smaller companies combine to compete against the larger ones.

As we have seen already in chapter 2, there are several options as far as *manipulation* is concerned. These involve the decision whether to coerce, induce, persuade, or obligate and will not be discussed further here.

Whether to Act Within the Existing Political Structure or to Expand the Structure

Until now the discussion has implicitly assumed that the firm has accepted the status quo and has confined itself to acting in the existing system.   This is not necessarily the case.   The firm may well attempt to create new elements in the system.

By creating *new* political relations, the firm may be able to effect indirect manipulation of symbionts or commensals.

- For example, many firms that are facing situations of increasing government regulation have the choice of remaining in the industry (where they are almost powerless against the increasing demands of government agencies, however damaging to profits these demands may be) or of trying to find new areas of activity where they do not have the power balance so decidedly to their disadvantage.   Many companies that traditionally supplied such industries are diversifying into other less controlled industries.

If we take these four dimensions of possible action (and remove those that are mutually exclusive), it is possible to identify twelve major options which are available to the firm contemplating political action.   These are depicted in Table 6.1.

Table 6.1.   Representation of General Options Available to the Political Strategist.

Political Relations

Symbionts	Direct	Accommodation	Existing
		Manipulation	Existing
	Indirect	Accommodation	Existing
			New
		Manipulation	Existing
			New
Commensals	Direct	Accommodation	Existing
		Manipulation	Existing
	Indirect	Accommodation	Existing
			New
		Manipulation	Existing
			New

In addition, Table 6.2 indicates the major suboptions available as far as manipulative and accommodative choices are concerned.

It is obviously impossible to detail the actions that can take place in a specific situation, unless the circumstances of the situation are known.   However, the number of symbionts and commensals in the environment is a major determinant of what actions may or may not be feasible.   Symbiont/commensal relations are discussed next.

Table 6.2. Manipulative and Accommodative Suboptions.

Accommodation	Joint commitment Co-optation Coalescence
Manipulation	Coercion Inducement Obligation Persuasion

NUMBER OF SYMBIONT/COMMENSAL RELATIONS AS MAJOR DETERMINANTS OF POLITICAL OPTIONS

The political action that the firm undertakes in its environment depends largely on the relative number of symbionts and commensals in the environment.   The number of each can be arbitrarily classed as *many* or *few*, and a simple representation of these conditions has been given as in Table 6.3.

Table 6.3. Major Conditions under Which the Firm Must Take Political Action in Its Environment.

		Commensals	
		Few	Many
Symbionts	Few	Bilateral Oligopoly	Oligopsony
	Many	Oligopoly	Perfect Competition

By *few* we mean more than one symbiont or at least one commensal. *Many*, on the other hand, is some arbitrary amount larger than, say twenty, after which coordination and control of joint action becomes difficult.

The few commensals/few symbionts condition corresponds to the bilateral oligopoly situation in economics.   The few commensals/many symbionts condition corresponds to an oligopoly situation. The many commensals/few symbionts situation corresponds to the oligopsony situation. The many commensals/many symbionts situation corresponds to a perfect competition situation.

Each situation in Table 6.3 gives rise to distinctive limits to the types of political action the firm *can* use.

In the next section the political options of the firm under each of these four conditions will be discussed.

It is possible (MacMillan 1972) to discuss in some detail the ways in which the structure of symbionts and commensals limits the options and suboptions of political action available to the firm under each of the four conditions depicted in Table 6.3. This would be very tedious, and the purposes of this book will not be served by such a detailed and long-winded analysis.

Instead, the major options available to a firm under various environmental conditions have been indicated in Table 6.4. It should be noted that many of the options listed draw on economics and marketing concepts as well as political concepts. The purpose here is to present a general array of possible options that could be considered in contemplation of interorganizational political action.

Table 6.4 has been found to be a useful vehicle for identifying the broad thrust that could be employed in developing a political strategy under different environmental conditions.

Thus, reading down Table 6.4 indicates where the main thrust of political action could be made in each (simplified) environment. For instance, a firm operating in an environment with many symbionts and few commensals (column 2 of Table 6.4) could develop a political strategy which has the following theme (once again these options should only be considered if legal in the country of reference):

1. Attempt to create a legal or pseudo-legal system for obtaining joint commitments of commensals to issues that tend to disrupt the industry.

2. If the company is a smaller one in the industry, be alert to opportunities to merge with commensals or form consortia with other smaller commensals in order to handle the challenge of the larger ones.

3. Be prepared to reduce disruptive conflict between commensals by developing a suitable system of side payments for adhering to stabilizing agreements.

4. Develop a basis on which to threaten uncooperative commensals.

Table 6.4. Key Options for Political Strategy under Major Environmental Conditions.

	1. Many Commensals/ Many Symbionts (Perfect Competition)	2. Few Commensals/ Many Symbionts (Oligopoly)	3. Many Commensals/ Few Symbionts (Oligopsony)	4. Few Commensals/ Few Symbionts (Bilateral Oligopoly)
Action Toward Commensals				
Direct Accommodation	Joint commitment via industry association; coalescence via merger of commensals	Joint commitment via pseudo-legal agreements; coalescence of smaller commensals by merger or consortia	Joint commitment via industry associations; coalescence via acquisition of less efficient commensals	Joint commitment via industry association and pseudo-legal agreements; coalescence of smaller commensals by mergers or consortia
Direct Manipulation		Inducement via side payments; coercion via threats; controlled erosion of commensals' power position		Inducements via side payments; coercion via threats; controlled erosion of commensal power base
Indirect Accommodation		Develop signaling systems to stabilize industry		Develop signaling systems to stabilize industry
Indirect Manipulation		Seek indirect power and influence; seek new domains to reduce threat base of commensals		Actively seek indirect power and influence; seek new domains to reduce threat base of commensals
Action Towards Symbionts				
Direct Accommodation	Joint commitment via contracting	Joint commitment via contracting	Joint commitment via contracting, co-optation of symbionts	Joint commitment via contracting; vertical integration; co-optation of symbionts
Direct Manipulation	Inducement via specialization in a narrow segment; persuasion and obligation via influence with target segment	Inducement via continuous differentiation of offering; coercion of controlled symbionts; persuasion via mass communication; investments in publicity, philanthropy; intelligence systems	Inducement via specialization with specific symbionts; persuasion via personal contacts; obligation via co-opted symbionts	Inducement via specialization development; persuasion via personal contact; obligation via commitment of customers to product; investment in intelligence systems
Indirect Accommodation				Develop signaling systems to stabilize industry
Indirect Manipulation	Persuasion and obligation via influence over indirect symbionts		Appeals to regulatory bodies; development to new domains to reduce symbiont dependance	Seek new domains to reduce threat base of symbionts

5. Formulate a strategy whereby the power base of the commensals is eroded rather than directly attacked, using the threat base and side payments to prevent retaliating action from commensals.

6. Develop a system of *implicit* signals that will be used to signal orderly changes in variables that could lead to disruptive action (for example, price leadership patterns, once recognized, prevent calamitous price wars).

7. Devote effort to analyzing and identifying major dependencies between commensals and their symbionts so that their strengths and weaknesses are exposed.

8. Attempt to reduce the company's vulnerability to threats from commensals by developing new relations that either enhance the power and influence of the firm in the current situation or reduce the dependence of the firm on the current situation.

9. Use the power position of the company to secure favorable contracts from symbionts.

10. Invest funds that will ensure the continuous differentiation of the firm's offering from that of competitors.

11. Develop a subgroup of controlled symbionts.

12. Invest funds in the development of audience via mass communication, publicity, and philanthropy.

13. Invest funds in the development of intelligence systems that will track shifts in symbionts' perceptions and values, as well as commensals actions.

This general strategy is substantially different from the one that could be adopted by conditions of columns 1, 3, or 4 of Table 6.4.

There are several caveats to be noted with Table 6.4.

1. The list of options is by no means exhaustive.

2. The table represents a substantial oversimplification of environmental structure. The dichotomy of "few" and "many" leaves a lot of room for interpretation. However, the intention is to indicate where the main emphasis in political strategy formulation could be made.

3. *In all cases, you should not assume that illegal action is being suggested. Each option indicated should be treated strictly in terms of the specific legal constraints imposed by the society in which the reader operates.*

4. Table 6.4 represents a single symbiont/firm/commensal relation. Since there are many such relations, it is possible that some of

the actions suggested above could not be undertaken, in which case they would be excluded from the strategy.

5. Table 6.4 only provides the general options for a political strategy. Whether a specific option is viable is a function of the expected response of elements in the environment. These expected responses can be developed by applying the concepts of strategic anticipation, to be discussed below.

STRATEGIC ANTICIPATION

The guidelines for strategic anticipation will draw heavily on the works of two authors, Allison (1971) and Thompson (1967), who in turn have used many other authors' contributions in the development of their arguments.

Allison discusses the ways in which complex strategic decisions are made from the perspective of three distinct but not mutually exclusive models: the rational actor model, the organizational process model, and the bureaucratic political model. The emphasis in this book has been on the political model, but it is useful when considering strategic responses from our opponents to think in terms of the other models as well.

With the *rational actor* model, we conceive of our opponent as a rational unitary decision maker with a clear set of goals who perceives our strategic moves clearly, generates a clear set of alternative actions, and selects the alternative on a rational basis.

•   For instance, the arguments which were used to develop Table 6.4 above were based on the rational actor model. We tried to indicate what an organization could do in launching a political strategy, assuming that the organization is acting "rationally."

With the *organizational process* model we conceive of an opponent as a group of departments held together in the organization and coordinated by a series of rules, procedures, policies, and programs. The decisions that the organization makes will be determined by the particular perspectives of the different departments, each with their own narrow perspective of the problem, their own set of goals, and their own desired choices. It may not be possible for the organization to perceive the whole problem, but only to perceive parts of it, depending on the perceptions of the various departments.

- For instance, a strategic move that we make to secure control of a specific segment of the market such as the "youth market" may influence sales of the product marginally over many geographic areas. If the competitors monitor sales by geographic region only, each geographic division tracking its sales over time, then the overall impact on their total sales may be small enough to be dismissed as a temporary aberration in sales. Further, if these figures are only collated by quarter, it may take several months before they are even aware of our inroads. In the meantime, we may have had the opportunity to consolidate our position.

The *bureaucratic political* model takes a perspective that we have used in this book. The decision-making organization is viewed as a series of coalitions in the organization, each with a leader who has to represent the interests of the coalition. Decision making is thus characterized by political perspectives as each coalition leader views the possible alternative action in terms of how it will affect the power and influence structure of the organization and the impact on him as a member of the coalition, as a member of the organization, and as a person.

In the rest of this chapter, the implications of these models for strategic anticipation are discussed.

OPPONENT AS A RATIONAL ACTOR

As was stated above, the one way of anticipating strategic response is to consider the opponent as a rational actor. We think of the way in which "the company" or "the union" or "the Department of Labor" would respond, as if the organization were a single, purposive person with specific goals in mind. The extent to which our strategic moves affect these goals will determine whether a counterresponse can be expected and what the likely counterresponse will be.

This perspective is important for two reasons.

1. Some organizations—generally small ones, or ones in which most of the decision making is done by a very powerful and small number of people at the top—will tend to act "as if" individual decisions are being made.

2. On many occasions we would like to structure conditions so that organizations *do* act "rationally."

The essence of using the rational actor model is to put ourselves in the position of the opponent facing our strategic move and to try to determine what the most rational counterresponses would be.

However, in order to be able to do this, we need to have as clear an idea as possible of the following:

Opponents' Objective Set

What goals are they seeking and which goals are being pursued with emphasis? Where is the current focus? How are these goals traded off against one another?

- If the organization we are moving against appears to be aggressively seeking market share and deemphasizing profits, then a move on our part that threatens to have an immediate and highly visible impact on market share may elicit an immediate and aggressive response. Ways of making the move that are less obvious and have less immediate impact are likely not to be countered as aggressively. A firm in the travel industry announced its intentions of getting into a certain country with tours comparable to the ones in which an established company dominated, and sought to maintain, market share. This announcement was, within days, met by reduction in prices and an increase in quality of existing tours by the dominant company, which was prepared to prune its profits considerably just to maintain its dominant position. However, if the aggressor had investigated further, it would have found that the dominant firm was concentrating its efforts only in the northern areas of the country. The new firm could have focused its initial efforts in the south, where the dominant firms' current business was obtained without direct marketing. The response of the dominant firm would have been much more restrained if the aggressor had focused initially in the South.

Opponents' Strategy

What are the major policy commitments that the opponent has made as to products, markets, distribution channels, promotion methods, and pricing? Where are the major shares of discretionary income being directed? To research, development, marketing, equipment? How are key personnel rewarded? What type of people are promoted? The point here is that the organization develops a momentum on the basis of the strategy it formulates, and this highly coordinated and massive movement of resource flows is difficult to redirect without a great deal of disruption. In the face of a strategic move that would make this redirection necessary, the opponent may decide to forgo the opportunity to counter this strategy.

- An electronics equipment manufacturer developed a strategy in which it dominated the market through the development of high-quality, extremely reliable sophisticated equipment based on new technology. Initial users required these product characteristics, but only until they themselves had come to grips with the new technology. Over time, user competence rose to the level that they could handle many of the problems of less expensive, lower-quality but much cheaper equipment themselves. However, the manufacturer was unwilling to "abandon its quality strategy." The entire organization was geared to produce quality. Its investments in equipment, its technicians and managers, its contracts with suppliers all supported a quality product and, for this to be changed, massive efforts in developing new processes, buying new machinery and redeveloping employees would have been necessary. Therefore, the response to the advent of lower-quality price competitors was to allow them slowly to erode market share.

Opponents' Long-term Resource Commitment

What major investments is the opponent making? What is the structure of its immobile assets? Who and what type of training is taking place? What major long-term contracts must it meet? What type of technology is it pursuing?

The point here is that long-range commitments take a long time to bear fruition and a great deal of funds and resources are tied up for considerable periods of time before profits start being generated. To terminate such commitments and redeploy the resources takes a great deal of courage, for not only does this often mean a total loss of all that has gone before but the process of readjustment can be extremely painful. The less accustomed to such decisions the opponent may be, the more likely it is that they will persist in the course that has been set some years before in the hope that "things will turn out all right in the end."

- Consider the case in which a building contractor waited until its major competitor was overcommitted on contracts before moving into the segment dominated by the major competitor. At that point all attention in the target organization was focused on coping with the large overload of contracts. When the aggressor did move, it focused its emphasis primarily on its ability to deliver contracts on time—at a stage when the target was powerless to respond in kind because it was overloaded and late on deliveries already.
- Another equipment manufacturer invested most of its resources in staying ahead of competition in a certain technology. Its major competitor, which was much smaller than it, made a breakthrough in a less advanced technology and has since that date been systematically consolidating its position and increasing its share of the market while it catches up on the ad-

vanced technology. To this day, the manufacturer has persisted in pursuing the advanced technology at enormous cost in the hope that once the breakthrough comes it will reestablish dominance. Every month, the decision to abandon the advanced technology becomes more painful and difficult to make.

So, with some concept of the opponent's objectives, strategy, and long-term resource deployments, it is possible to "put ourselves in the shoes" of the opponent and try to decide what responses the opponent could make when faced with a strategic move on our part.

We are in a position to determine what alternatives the opponent *could* choose.

In the next two models, we try to determine what factors would influence the decisions it *would* choose.

OPPONENT AS AN ORGANIZATION

In chapter 5 we briefly focused on the problems of coordinating a complex organization facing a complex environment. To do this, the organization subdivides itself into specialist parts that handle specific subtasks relating to keeping the organization effective, efficient, or adaptable in the face of environmental demand.

However, by the very fact that it *does* subdivide, the organization creates for itself problems of ensuring that the many separate subtasks are coordinated and controlled.

1. The organization must coordinate the disparate demands for resources and ensure that the transfer of these resources from one department to another or from one subdepartment to another actually takes place; otherwise, instead of absorbing uncertainty, these departments *create* uncertainties for one another. This coordination problem of the organization results in the development of a large number of "bureaucratic" rules, procedures, policies, and programs whereby the departments are instructed how to act under an array of specified conditions.

2. The organization must also *control* the activities of its departments to ensure that they (a) do not single-mindedly pursue their own subtasks to the detriment of the organization as a whole and (b) carry out these subtasks. In order to cope with this problem, the organization develops complex control systems that monitor the performance of the divisions, assess the performance and then reward or punish the division according to how well the task has been performed.

The organizational process model recognizes that the possible response of an opponent is influenced by these bureaucratic processes in many ways.

First, if the strategic move we make is something that the opponent has never encountered before (as is often the case), it does not *have* a set of rules, policies, or procedures to cater to this move. In many cases it may respond to the move by continuing as it has always done or perhaps by countering the move in the nearest way it can find that "fits the rules." In particular, *policies* that emerge as the guidelines for behavior in response to demands from powerful internal and external interest groups are difficult to change, and there is a tendency for the organizations to persist in these policies.

- For instance, a company may have committed itself to a policy of maintaining a specific liquidity level as a result of demands from its creditors and can find itself in a very difficult position if the move we make demands that they counter by redeploying cash and thus reducing liquidity.

Second, procedures and rules by which the organization monitors or "sees" its environment may be such that they fail to notice the move we have made.

- The example we used above in which a company decided to go for the youth market and went unnoticed because its competitor did not have a category in its sales analysis called "youth market" is of relevance here.

Third, the *time* that it takes for information about the move to reach the decision-making level where a counterresponse *can* be generated can cause critical delays.

- For example, a young woman used to "blitzkreig" different areas of the household chemicals market at different times. By the time the head office of the competitors received information concerning her inroads, it was too late to respond, because she had already moved out of that region and into the next one.

Fourth, the way in which the organization assesses performance may influence whether the signal gets to the decision-making level that generates the response at all and in what form it gets there.

- Thompson (1967) has argued that organizations (or their parts) will provide information on which they are assessed in forms that suit them rather than not. Hence, if one is losing market share in a growth market one will tend to prefer to be assessed on historical sales growth rather than market share. One may, therefore choose to report historical growth rather than growth compared with one's competitors.

Fifth, in designing the coordination of resources between divisions, the organization must make commitments of resources. It is therefore disruptive if a particular division makes sudden demands for these resources. This disrupts the pattern that has been planned, and it can create critical delays.

Sixth, the specific perspective of one department (say sales) may make them rather unsympathetic to problems encountered in another department (say production) and this lack of perspective on both parts often gives rise to parochial conflicts and conflicts of jurisdiction and authority as *each* department tries to "solve" the problem posed by the strategic move in terms of *its* frame of reference.

Therefore, in formulating some sense of the type of responses we can expect from our opponents, it is important that we consider the following.

What types of major rules, procedures, policies, and programs are used by opponents? These may influence the visibility of our move and the time it takes to recognize the move and limit the responses they can generate.

What major monitoring and control systems does the opponent employ? How are departments evaluated? How often are they measured? How are people rewarded and punished? At what level in the organization are decisions relevant to our move made?

How is the opponent organized? What major departments does it have? Will the strategic move directly affect more than one department? Will it affect them in different ways? Are there likely to be conflicts between departments? How ingrained are the systems in these departments? What constraints are imposed on their actions by the organization?

The better the knowledge we have of these factors, the better we can assess the impact of strategic moves that we contemplate and the likely responses to them, given the time lags and coordination problems that would be experienced in the opponent as a result of the move.

- For example, many banks and insurance companies can only survive on the basis of very detailed rules, procedures, and programs and, after many years of operating with them, the employees become conditioned to respond to problems only in terms of "the book." When a new bank was launched in such an industry, the bank's chief executive developed his marketing strategy on the basis of better personal service to the customer, but in dramatic ways. His banks stayed open longer hours and had personnel who were specifically assigned to assist customers with unusual problems, and he allowed considerably more discretion to branch managers as far as loans were concerned. He employed field salespeople to go out and secure accounts by offering slightly better credit facilities than the competition. The competing banks were paralyzed against this strategy by virtue of not having *anyone* in their organization who could work under those conditions. No one wanted to work longer hours, no one felt obliged to give personal attention to customers, the branch managers were unable to handle extra discretion and those that were given it did not use it, and no one knew how to go out and solicit accounts. In a matter of two years the bank became a national force in the market. The competitors wasted many man-hours of effort *just in jurisdictional disputes* between various departments as to who was to handle the strategic responses to this brash new competitor.

- The same type of thing happened in the home appliance market of a certain country. Retailers, large and small, had settled into a comfortable coexistence where prices were held steady and competition was largely in terms of credit facilities, ever-increasing service and maintenance guarantees, and special features. A young entrepreneur managed to break the suppliers' fear of retribution from the big chains of retailers and secure supply lines. He then came into the market with the same appliances, but at high discounts for cash, with no credit, with sound guarantees but no service. Once again, it took two years for the competitors to break the paralysis caused by the fact that they had many resources committed to their service guarantees and their store managers and personnel had been conditioned, and rewarded, *not* to encourage low-cost cash deals. The entire reward system had to be reworked to cater for cash as well as financed deals, and while this was being done, to the accompaniment of much demoralization, the entire system of rules, policies, and programs had to be revamped. This was accompanied by jurisdictional disputes, because it must be remembered that the big retailers had many lines *other* than appliances and the new set of rules and procedures had to cater equitably for all lines. In the end the newcomer emerged with a solid share of the national market.

The organizations that are particularly vulnerable to bureaucratic processes are large, widely dispersed ones that have had a period of stability in the industry.

Analysis of the organizational processes of the opponent thus unfolds many alternatives that they are *unlikely* to follow or unfolds facets of their operations that make a contemplated strategic move on our part less likely to be countered until we have a consolidated position.

OPPONENT AS A POLITICAL ENTITY

The last model follows the line of the theme we have seen in this book. It views the opponent as a political system in which powerful and influential interest groups, surrounding the organization or within it, place demands on the organization for the purpose of achieving their own purposes.

Key decision makers "see" the problem in terms of the interests they are expected (and conditioned) to represent, and any response is weighed in terms of the interests of the coalition to which these members belong.

This has an influence on how the organization *can* react. Certain alternatives which look "rational" in the economic sense would not be tolerated in the political context.

This descends to the level of a specific decision maker as well. The decision he must make will be influenced by (a) the extent to which it will be seen by his constituents as appropriate to their interests and (b) as Bower (1973) has pointed out, the riskiness of making an incorrect decision.

Thus, given an array of alternative responses, the specific decision maker, in choosing the specific response, must be aware of the political and personal risk involved and will tend to select on the basis of costs to him and his constituents of making an unsuccessful decision as well as the benefits of making a successful one.

As Bower points out, this need not be for self-seeking reasons, because the competence of a high-level decision maker carrying out a complex task can often only be judged in terms of their "track record" in such decision situations. A person who has a bad record for making complex decisions has less audience than one who has a good record, so every decision they make that can damage the track record risks future organizational support.

With this argument as a background, it is suggested that the opponent organization be analyzed in a political context. The analysis should seek some clarification of the following factors.

What is the Political Structure of the Organization?

Who are the dominant coalitions? What is their source of power and influence? Are there any major counter coalitions?

The results of this type of analysis will indicate the vulnerability of the organization to specific political moves. A political move could initiate a great deal of political activities within the organization if it is used as a "test of strength" by a major coalition. The analysis also will provide a sense of which alternative responses would be an anathema to the major interest groups and which would be more acceptable.

**What Major Demands Are
Being Placed on the Organization?**

Which interest groups are making these demands? How are inconsistent demands being handled? What generalized policy commitments have they made? To which commitments are they currently paying attention?

This analysis should provide a sense of what constraints are imposed on the organization and also what responses will be proscribed unless the organization can convince the relevant interest groups to relax the constraints. It also creates opportunities for the organization to distract the opponent by finding ways to highlight inconsistencies in the generalized policy commitments that have been made or to shift their attention to areas where the action of the strategist is less visible.

**What is the
Discretion Structure
in the Organization?**

Who can exercise discretion and at what level? How does the organization "treat" unsuccessful use of discretion?

A knowledge of these factors provides a sense of the riskiness of various responses to the opponents and the likelihood that some responses will not be considered because the proposal may be too risky for the proponent.

- For example, a certain cosmetics manufacturer waited until it knew that the marketing vice-president of its opponent had left on an extended vacation/overseas business trip before launching a new product line. The organization was paralyzed for several weeks while the stand-in vacillated, being unwilling to exercise his authority in the situation for fear of making the wrong move but reluctant to "contact the boss" for fear of not being up to the job.

The results of a political model perspective therefore give an indication of which responses are likely to be *acceptable* to the opponent. From this one is in a position to estimate the opponent's likely counterstrategies and select a strategy in such a way that their counterstrategies will prove less effective.

This concludes the discussion of strategic anticipation, and now all the elements that go into political strategy formulation have been covered. In the next chapter the formulation of political strategy will be discussed.

SUMMARY: KEY CONCEPTS

1.   The political strategist has a variety of options available in contemplating a political move. These can generally be classified in terms of four dichotomous dimensions:

> Whether to act towards symbionts or commensals;

> Whether to take direct or indirect action;

> Whether to manipulate or accommodate;

> Whether to act within the existing structure or create a new structure.

2.   Table 6.4 lists possible options for political action between organizations, given various numbers of symbionts and commensals in the situation.

3.   In anticipating the response of an opponent to a particular strategy, it is useful to analyse the opponent in terms of three models.

4.   Using the *rational action model,* one analyses the opponents objective set, its strategies and major policies and its long term resource commitments to estimate the responses it *could* make.

5.   Using the *organization process model,* one analyses the opponent's major rules, procedures and programs, its monitoring and control systems, its organization structure to determine which responses it is *unlikely* to be able to follow as a result of its bureaucritized nature.

6.   Using the *bureaucratic politics model,* one analyses the opponents political structure and dominant interest groups, the major demands being placed on the opponent, and its discretion structure to determine what responses are *acceptable* to the opponent.

7

Political Strategy Formulation

INTEGRATION OF MATERIAL

The purpose of this chapter is to use material from previous chapters to develop a framework for formulating political strategy. The procedure will be to indicate briefly the major phases that must be carried out in formulating political strategy, continually referring back to concepts that have been built up earlier in the book.

In the first part of the chapter the framework will be developed, based on a previous publication (MacMillan 1974).

In the next three chapters of the book, actual cases will be discussed, each one illustrating specific facets of the political strategy formulation processes.

Four main phases of political strategy formulation are identified:

1. Analysis of the total situation.
2. Identification of future threats and opportunities.
3. Political analysis.
4. Political strategy formulation.

Since the first two phases are essentially the same as those of Hofer and Schendel, the discussion of these phases will be abbreviated.

PRELIMINARY ANALYSIS
ANALYSIS OF THE TOTAL
SITUATION

The analysis of the total situation begins with a specification of the firm as a system interacting with its environment. A systematic identification of all the people, groups, or organizations on which the firm depends for its inputs is made, and this is schematically represented. At the same time the major competitors for these inputs are also identified and schematically represented.

Note that for political strategy formulation, this analysis has a wider scope than is normal for economic strategy formulation. Thus, instead of concentrating on a customer/market/product analysis, such symbionts as shareholders, employee groups, unions, competitors, and suppliers should also be analyzed and then examined for their possible impacts on the economic strategy.

In the next phase of the analysis, we need to project the trends which will be taking place in the firm's environment.

TREND ANALYSIS AND FORECASTING

Essentially the same types of trend analysis as are discussed in the Hofer and Schendel book should be carried out. This is done at three levels, the international/national level, the industry level, and the level of the organization itself.

However, in addition to identifying the trends associated with the firm itself, it is also important to identify trends associated with any of the major symbionts or commensals identified in the systems analysis discussed above.

Since this forecasting is discussed in detail in the Hofer and Schendel book, the topic will not be repeated here.

The implications of the above analyses are overlaid on the firm's current position. The object is to gain insight into how and where the firm depends most on its environment and what trends in these dependencies are likely to occur.

An analysis of the above trends in relation to the firm's activities will indicate where the future *threats to the firm's survival* and *outstanding opportunities* for its future might lie. Let us term these *critical decision areas*.

When identifying the critical decision areas, *identify those parts of the environment that pose the threat or opportunity,* for the identification of these critical elements in the environment is essential for the formulation of a political strategy.

IDENTIFICATION OF POTENTIAL ALLIES AND OPPONENTS

A political approach argues that the firm should actively attempt to structure the situation so as to promote its own goals. *It is pointless for the firm to strive towards these goals on its own if there are allies willing and able to help it.* These allies are found by identifying who else is going to be affected by the threats and opportunities it has identified. Any actor who is likely to be negatively affected by the threats is a potential ally. Any actor who is likely to benefit from the opportunities is a potential ally.

On the other hand, the actors who will suffer if the opportunity is seized by the firm form the potential opposition. Actors posing critical threats or those who stand to benefit from these threats are also potential opposition.

From the above analyses the following should emerge:

1. The critical threats to survival.
2. The outstanding opportunities open to the firm.
3. The potential allies in each critical decision area.
4. The potential opposition in each critical decision area.

POLITICAL ANALYSIS

OBJECT OF POLITICAL ANALYSIS

The object of political action is to structure or restructure the situation with the view of furthering one's own goals. A political analysis aims at identifying what the political capabilities (power and influence) of the various critical elements in the situation are.

The object of such a political analysis is to determine, for each potential ally or opponent, where it is dependent on its environment, for the more one can gain control of these dependencies, the more one can gain control of the actions of the relevant critical element. At the same time, the dependencies of the firm should be identified so that action can be taken to block similar maneuvers by the opposition.

In the following discussion of the process of political analysis only the broad theme of the analysis will be outlined, since the detailed considerations have been discussed earlier in the book and will be applied in the cases below.

ANALYSIS OF EXTERNAL POLITICAL CAPABILITY OF CRITICAL ELEMENTS

The first step in the political analysis involves determining the power and influence basis of the various critical elements. Here the application of the material in chapter 2 is required.

Identification of Input/Output Relations between Elements and Their Environment

This is done to determine what dependencies exist between the element and its environment. What should also be explored is the element's alternative structure—for which goods and services is it dependent and on whom is it dependent.

Identification of the Strategic Power and Influence Resources

By analyzing the dependencies of each critical element, we can get a sense of the strategic power and influence resources that will determine the behavior of the critical element. Areas of high dependency where there are few alternatives or where the marginal impact of single alternatives is high are important. Resources that could become critical in the future should be identified. Areas where the critical element has high commitments should be identified. Areas where the critical element has audience and possesses strategic information are indicators of the element's influence base (see chapter 2). Finally, areas where the element has formal authority should be identified.

Identification of External Coalition Structure

It is also important to get a sense of what interorganizational coalitions the critical element has joined and what issues gave rise to these coalitions. A change in the visibility or priority of these issues may disrupt the coalition.

Obviously, a similar analysis should be carried out for the firm itself. Once this has been done, it is appropriate to do an internal analysis of the critical element.

ANALYSIS OF THE INTERNAL POLITICAL STRUCTURE OF THE CRITICAL ELEMENTS

Here the concepts discussed in chapters 5 and 6 are applied, as follows:

Analysis of Objectives, Set, Strategy, and Longrange Resource Commitments

As we saw in chapter 6, this analysis gives us a sense of what constrains the organization's capacity to redirect its efforts and of what it considers to be important and worth fighting for. It also provides the basis for rationalizing any major moves it will be making.

Analysis of Organizational Processes

This analysis provides us with insights into the perspective from which various key decision makers within the organization view their environment and the shifts in that environment. It also gives us a sense of the rate at which the organization will respond to change, the amount of disruption such change could cause, the patterns of responses that could emerge from such change, and the level in the organization at which changes will be addressed.

Analysis of Political Structure

Here we are interested in what major external and internal interest groups are demanding of the critical element, who the dominant coalition members are, what major policy commitments have been made, and how and at what level discretion is employed and constrained by the politics of the system.

In our initial analysis, at least, many gaps in the information we desire will occur. Often it will be necessary to go without much of the above information, but it has been found that much of this information is available from members of the strategists' organization once the specific questions are asked. Where the information *is* lacking, effort could be devoted to obtaining the information.

IDENTIFICATION OF
STRENGTHS AND WEAKNESSES

The political systems of the critical elements are now analyzed in order to determine their strengths and weaknesses. This analysis should reveal whether they are highly dependent on parts of their environment, whether their internal political system is strained by internal conflict, whether their key personnel are dissatisfied with the ideology of the system, whether the structure of the system is so cumbersome that they cannot respond quickly to political maneuvering, whether their resources are at present immobilized by heavy commitments to others, and so on. Usually, a small number of important strengths and weaknesses of the critical elements are identified.

If interesting dependencies are identified, it may be worthwhile to carry the analysis even further and analyze the systems of these elements on whom the critical element is dependent. This will provide an indication of where indirect political action is possible.

The idea is *not* to become entangled thoroughly in a vast web of detailed and complex analyses, but to start at a broad level, to try to identify important factors, and then to pursue these factors in more detail.

INTEGRATION OF THE
POLITICAL ECONOMIC STRATEGY

By following the guidelines set by Hofer and Schendel, the firm will have developed an economic strategy aimed at securing a strong position in the marketplace. It cannot be stressed too strongly that the fundamental basis of long-run survival lies in a sound economic strategy, which strategy is the reason for the firm's very existence in society. So the purpose of the political strategy is to enhance and complement the economic strategy.

Use of the guidelines proposed by Hofer and Schendel will identify the specific strengths and weaknesses of the firm in an economic market context. From this will emerge the strategic decisions as to which opportunities and threats must be addressed by the firm in order for it to survive and prosper in the marketplace.

In *this* book we are not concerned with how these decisions are made. The opportunities and threats to be addressed are taken as given, and we proceed from the political analysis, assuming that the economic strategy has been determined. We proceed with political strategy formulation by asking how the environment is to be restructured in such a way that the success of the economic strategy is assured.

There is, however, one major caveat that is of relevance in this book. The proposed economic strategy must be assessed in terms of the internal political sytems of the firm proposing it.

The concepts developed in chapter 5 should therefore be applied in order to determine how the proposed economic strategy is going to integrate with the political processes of the firm. If the optimal economic strategy lacks internal support, it may be wiser to select a different but still viable strategy. If the optimal strategy will not be supported externally, the same argument applies. To help determine whether a proposed strategy is organizationally viable, the strategist should focus on the following questions.

Which Major Interest Groups in the Organization Are Effected by the Proposed Strategy and How?

A strategy cannot be successful without a high degree of commitment in the organization. It is inevitable that any major organizational changes are going to benefit some parts of the organization to the detriment of others. The strategist should be aware of which parts these are and get a sense of where resistances to the strategy will be experienced. He must then decide what must be done to ensure that the correct degree of commitment is obtained in the organization.

What Coalitions Are Likely to Form as a Result of the Strategy?

Strategic decisions raise issues in the organization that give rise to coalitions structured around these issues. The strategist should attempt to determine beforehand what coalitions will form and what the power and influence base of these coalitions are. If this is not done, the entire strategy could be aborted, with the result that (as we saw on the first page of chapter 2) a highly innovative chief executive might be "dumped" by a conservative board or a general manager might be forced to abandon a contemplated acquisition because of a coalition of rebellious subordinates. A prior estimate of the issues that are likely to arise and the power and influence of the coalitions that are likely to form gives the strategist the necessary foresight to preadapt to the expected conditions.

He can prepare for this in several ways—by adjusting the authority structure in subtle ways to reduce the power and influence of certain members, by formulating ahead of time the kinds of generalized policy commitments that will be necessary in order to obtain broader support, by determining ahead of time what sequential attention patterns will be necessary to maintain support as the strategy is launched and implemented, or by deciding what issues to make visible and what priorities to set on these issues, so that he can control some of the coalition formation in the organization. The larger and the more complex the organization, the more important it is that these factors be given consideration.

If the strategy being contemplated runs the risk of being subverted by internal dissension then it is inappropriate, however attractive it may be when viewed in an external context. The first actions should then be taken to make it *internally* appropriate.[1] Assuming that a strategy has been evolved in which the internal commitment is adequate, it is then possible to proceed with the formulation of political strategy.

POLITICAL STRATEGY FORMULATION

The economic strategy will have identified the outstanding opportunities that the firm has decided to pursue and the major threats that it intends to obviate.

The political analysis will have identified the critical elements that will be involved in pursuing these opportunities and in dealing with these threats. It will also have identified the strengths and weaknesses of the potential allies, of the potential opposition, and of the firm itself.

ESTABLISHING INDEPENDENT CAPABILITY

As a first step, the strengths and weaknesses of the firm and its opposition should be matched against one another to determine, roughly, the firm's political capability vis-a-vis its opposition.

From this matching process the firm obtains a general idea of its capacity to cope with the critical decision areas *independently*. The scope of its *individual* capability is therefore established.

---

[1] We do not need to have *total* commitment, but we need to have *sufficient* internal commitment for success. There often will be parts of the organization that will be dissatisfied with the strategy. We must ensure that they do not endanger the strategy by their lack of commitment.

This is important, since it provides an assessment of what the firm can do *without* allies and thus lays the groundwork for clearly determining the bargaining base in future negotiations with potential allies.

ALLIANCE SELECTION

Knowing its capacity to cope with a situation on its own, the firm is now in a position to set tentative objectives in respect to the position that it hopes to reach by acting independently against the opposition. These tentative objectives form the basis of the firm's decisions on the selection of allies. Since the independent political capability of the firm itself constitutes the "bargaining base" of the firm in subsequent negotiations with allies, it will accept no agreement with allies that will cause it to achieve less than it would by acting on its own.

For the next step the firm must select a combination of allies for each critical decision area. The combined strengths and weaknesses of the final alliance must be matched against the strengths and weaknesses of the opposition. At the same time, the firm's political capability vis-a-vis the members of the alliance must be assessed.

The firm must cope with a whole set of critical decision areas. An ally that is useful in one critical decision area may prove incompatible with another area. So the firm's problem is to determine the *best set of allies* for its total strategy. This can be done by means of a cyclic procedure. A combination of allies is selected, and the compatibility with the firm's objectives is assessed. If they are compatible, the firm assesses, first, the extent to which the alliances it forms for each critical decision area can cope with those of the opposition in that critical decision and, second, the extent to which the firm can cope with the alliance.

The goals of the firm and its allies will not be perfectly congruent. The firm should, therefore, identify and list the *major issues* that will arise in the alliance.

If these issues will cause incompatibilities between the firm and a potential ally, that ally is disqualified. After a few alternative alliances have been considered, a best alliance usually can be selected.

In the next step, the firm must negotiate with the potential allies to form the alliance. At this stage the firm should consider the options at its disposal. Depending on the structures of symbionts or commensals in the situation, the firm should review the contents of Figure 6.4, which lays out the options usually available, and undertake political action to ensure that the best possible conditions prevail for itself before it enters alliance formation.

The firm then undertakes political action against the potential allies, attempting to structure the situation in such a way that the agreements to be reached with alliance members will turn out best for the firm. However, since it wants to reach agreement with the allies, it can ill afford to alienate them. At the same time there are a number of issues on which there will not be initial agreement.

Alliance negotiation therefore involves maintaining a very delicate balance between achieving as much for the firm as possible but not endangering the alliance by being greedy. The major manipulative tools at this stage tend to be persuasion and inducement rather than coercion and obligation.

ALLIANCE NEGOTIATIONS

For negotiations that are critical to the strategic future of the firm, a well-prepared negotiating strategy is essential. Here the concepts of negotiating strategy and tactics developed in chapter 3 should be applied. The most important of these are:

Identification of Major Negotiation Issues Which Will Arise, accompanied by an analysis of the stand to be taken on these issues, in terms of the priority of such issues for ourselves and the estimated priority for our opponents.

Indentification of Critical Issues and the key bluffs, threats, and promises that we shall use or expect the opponent to use.

Specification of Desired Agenda, which should be structured in such a way that differences in issue priorities between us and opponents can be used to advantage by us.

Information Gathering about the potential allies, particularly concerning their previous tactics, the context in which they make decisions, the alternatives they have, and who their key decision makers are.

Identification of Critical Stages at which the process may need reassessment as missing information about the opponents is obtained.

Development of a Negotiating Theme which will be used to tie the arguments together and support the key bluffs, threats, and promises required in handling the issues.

Establishment of Checkpoints and Objectives by which the firm's negotiators can assess their performance as each stage of the negotiation is concluded.

The firm should then negotiate an alliance and, subject to the results of this negotiation, reset the tentative objectives. It can now set about developing the political strategies that it and the alliance will bring to bear against the opposition.

FORMULATION OF OFFENSIVE AND DEFENSIVE STRATEGIES

With the formation of the alliance, new information regarding the strengths and weaknesses of the allies and the opposition may be brought in and it may be necessary to modify the firm's original assessments of the alliance's strengths and weaknesses.

The alliance now develops an *offensive strategy* (a) to exploit the opposition's weaknesses and (b) to erode the opposition's strengths, and it simultaneously develops a *defensive strategy* for countering the opposition's attempts to (a) exploit the alliance's weaknesses and (b) to erode the alliance's strengths.

If, as is usual, the opposition is strong, then inevitably the alliance will have to negotiate with them. In this case, the alliance should first attempt to manipulate the situation by using the power and influence at its disposal and then to accommodate by bargaining. This sequencing must be taken into account when strategies are being formulated.

In formulating the offensive and defensive strategies, the strategist must bear in mind these aspects:

1. The strategist should try to arrange action when his strategic resources are as high as possible and the opponent's are as low as possible. This factor could necessitate delaying action until the time is right.
2. A solid knowledge of the key decision makers in the opposition. It is important to remember that, ultimately, opposition's responses are the results of decisions made *by people*. Therefore, once the general focus of the political strategy has been determined, we need to know how the key people in the situation will be affected.
3. Once again, a strategy is not unilateral. The opposition can be expected to respond. The rational actor, organization process, and political models in chapter 6 should be used in order to develop and anticipate the strategic responses of the opposition.

Once the strategies have been formulated, detailed plans may be developed and monitoring systems evolved to evaluate the effectiveness of these plans.

The political strategy can then be initiated and will be continuously monitored and updated by both the alliance and the firm as time progresses. The results of this monitoring process constitute the input for the reinitiation of the strategy formulation process.

In order to place the above discussion in an applied perspective, practical illustrations of how a political strategy was developed in a number of situations is given in chapters 8, 9, and 10.

Hence there will be no key concepts summarizing this chapter.

8

Illustrative Case Study: Alpha Oil Mills

The next three chapters are devoted to analyses of cases illustrating political strategy formulation. Each case has been selected because it highlights specific facets of the political strategy process. No one case makes use of all the concepts considered in this book. It is impossible, even in three cases, to illustrate all the concepts discussed; however, they have all proved useful at one time or another.

Before the illustrative cases are discussed, some caveats and qualifications are given.

1. In the illustrative cases below, space limitations demand that a simplified situation be described. The purpose of the cases is to illustrate, not to provide a complete case history. It is an attempt to convey the key concepts in developing a political strategy.[1]

2. It so happens that the first case involves national politics. This need not have been the case: the activities of the firm are political in the sense defined above and not in the national political sense, as we shall see in the next two cases. What the first case does

---

[1] In the interest of keeping the confidence of the companies who have participated in the development of this book, their names, products, and/or countries have been disguised. The cases and examples in this book are illustrative, and one should not make assumptions based on similarities that one sees between the case material and specific companies.

117

underline, however, is that the concepts of political strategy developed in this book *do* have applications up to the level of national politics.

3. Please note that in not one of the cases below does the company involved formulate a political strategy that is in direct conflict with the public interest. Political strategy can (and should) be employed in ways that do not involve illegal or immoral activities.

THE PROBLEM OF ALPHA OIL MILLS [2]

In 1966, Alpha Oil Mills, a producer of edible oils, after having carried out an analysis of the total situation along the lines described above, has identified a single outstanding opportunity—to manufacture margarine.

Figure 8.1. The Initial Analysis of the Oilseed Industry.

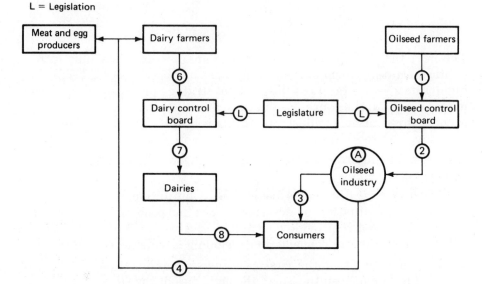

Source. "Business Strategies for Political Action," *Journal of General Management,* vol. 2, no. 1, Autumn 1974. Reprinted by permission.

Alpha is located in an agricultural country that suffered severely during the depression years, during which the powerful dairy farm

[2] The Alpha Oil Mills Case has been briefly discussed in a previous publication. (MacMillan 1974).

lobby in the government had succeeded in prohibiting the sale of butter substitutes. Thus, in 1966, margarine sales are prohibited by legislation. Dairy product sales are carefully monitored by a dairy control board—a semiautonomous government body instituted to protect the interests of the dairy farmers. Alpha, however, is intent on manufacturing margarine, because it has tremendous potential.

Alpha is part of the oilseed-processing industry (Figure 8.1). This industry in general obtains oilseed from oilseed farmers (1), via an oilseed control board (2), another semiautonomous government body instituted to protect the interests of the oilseed farmers. The oilseeds are processed to form cooking oils and fats, which are sold (3) to consumers (the distribution system is ignored for the example).

Meal, a by-product of the oil-recovery process, is made into animal feeds and sold (4) to meat producers, egg producers, and dairy farmers. Butter is produced by dairy farmers and channeled (6) via the auspices of the dairy control board to dairies (7) and thence to the final consumer (8).

This then is the situation in which Alpha finds itself.

The critical elements that Alpha identified were the competitors, the consumers, the dairy farmers, the dairy control board, the meat and egg producers, the consumers, the oilseed control board, and the oilseed farmers.

Potential allies are the competitors and the consumers who would all benefit by the introduction of margarine. Potential opponents are the dairy farmers and the dairy control board.

POLITICAL ANALYSIS
OF THE ALPHA OIL MILLS SYSTEM

The external political systems of the firm and of the critical elements are now identified and overlaid in diagram form. Particular attention is paid to the inclusion of those relations in which the critical elements are highly dependent on or highly committed to parts of their environment. Many of the relations between the critical elements and their environment are irrelevant to the situation at hand and can be discarded.

Finally, a diagram such as Figure 8.2 is obtained in which the most important relations between the critical elements and their environment are overlaid on the political system of the firm.

Figure 8.2.   Expanded Analysis of the Oilseed Industry.

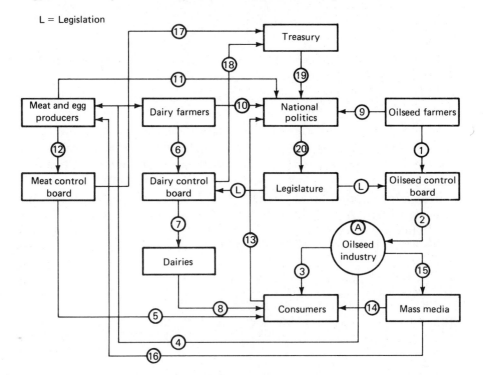

Source: "Business Strategies for Political Action," *Journal of General Management,*
vol. 2, no. 1, Autumn 1974. Reprinted by permission.

In the example, the most important relations are the following.
The oilseed farmers are a significant lobbying group in national
politics (9), as are the dairy farmers (10) and the meat and egg farmers (11). Meat and egg producers supply their products (12) to the
same type of control boards as the dairy and oilseed industries. The
meat and egg control boards distribute the products to consumers (5).
The consumers' attitudes play a role in national politics (13). These
attitudes are influenced by mass media (14), which could possibly be
used by the oilseed industry (15) to influence consumers and the
meat and egg producers (16). In addition to internal sales, the control boards are responsible for exporting their constituents' products
(or importing them in times of shortage). Its activities are keenly
observed by the Treasury (17 and 18) concerned with problems of
balance of payments.

Efficient and low-cost meat and egg production is essential if
the country is to compete in world export markets. If meat produc-

tion costs can be reduced, then consumers will be very satisfied and export prices will be more acceptable to world markets. The treasury will gain valuable foreign revenue if meat exports can be increased.

Butter shortages cause butter imports, which in turn cause increased foreign expenditure (18). This is an anathema to the treasury, which has a significant say in national politics (19). National politics results in legislation (20).

One of the ways of reducing meat and egg costs is for producers to enter industrialized farming. This necessitates the use of animal feeds, but the problem with animal feeds is that they are very expensive. The profits from sales of edible oil and cooking fat are relatively low. With minimal additional investment Alpha could produce large quantities of margarine at a price substantially below that of butter and still make very good profits. As things stand, they have to maintain high feed prices because the profits on oil and fats are depressed.

If the restriction on margarine could be removed or relaxed, some of the profits of margarine production could be diverted to paying higher prices for oilseeds on the one hand and charging lower prices for feed meals on the other. However, this process is being impeded by the dairy control board, acting under the regulations imposed by the dairy control bill.

As a result of the political analysis, more potential allies have been identified. The potential allies of Alpha are now the other oilseed processors, the oilseed control board, the oilseed farmers, the meat and egg control boards, the meat and egg producers, and the treasury. With the political analysis of the system taken care of, it is now possible to proceed with an analysis of strengths and weaknesses of the opposition.

ANALYSIS OF THE STRENGTHS AND WEAKNESSES OF THE OPPOSITION

STRENGTHS OF OPPOSITION

The major strength of the opposition is that the dairy control board is semi-autonomous body which has full authority regarding sales of all dairy products and their substitutes. Their autonomy is protected by legislation, and it is an extremely lengthy and frustrating business to have legislation changed.

The other major strength is the significant lobbying power of the farmers in national politics, who usually support one another en bloc. However, by *refocusing on issues* of oilseed and meal prices it may be possible to divide the farmers into two opposing coalitions—dairy farmers versus egg, meat, and oilseed farmers.

WEAKNESSES OF OPPOSITION

Butter production is highly dependent on climatic conditions. In years of drought, butter demand exceeds supply and butter has to be imported at great cost, causing a drain on foreign currency reserves. The treasury would prefer this not to happen. In these periods, butter prices increase substantially, which is hard on the consumers.

Butter production costs are high, and butter is expensive. Many sectors of the general public would prefer to have margarine.

In years of drought there is an increased demand for animal feeds.

Given this assessment of strengths and weaknesses the firm must set tentative objectives to determine what it can do on its own.

The firm is virtually powerless on its own. It needs the support of the entire edible-oil industry if the situation is to be changed. Therefore, it cannot set tentative objectives for acting *independently*. It can, however, set the constraint that it get at least a "fair share" of what any alliance accomplishes.

It is compelled to resort to the use of allies, so the strengths and weaknesses of the potential allies must be identified.

POTENTIAL ALLIES

STRENGTHS OF POTENTIAL ALLIES

Margarine is cheaper than butter, which will mean that, if the consumers as a group could be politically activated, a great deal of pressure could be exerted on the national political structure. This will require the support of the media.

Meat and egg producers would have a significant lobbying power in national politics if they could be politically activated.

Oilseed farmers would have a significant lobbying power if they could be politically activated.

The other control boards have leverage that they could use against the dairy control board.

WEAKNESSES OF POTENTIAL ALLIES

Consumers are politically apathetic.

The oilseed processors have very little lobbying power in national politics.

It may be difficult to politically motivate the other potential allies.

The selection of the first alliance would follow the line of argument below:

The firm should obviously ally itself with other oilseed producers in order to present a united front to other critical elements. However, with the limited lobbying power they have it is unlikely that they will accomplish much more than the firm alone. Therefore, a broader alliance must be sought.

It is unlikely that the oilseed farmers and consumers can be activated without extensive persuasive efforts. If they are to be activated, the media must be brought in. The meat producers may be interested in lobbying for margarine products if this means that cheaper feeds will be available.

The first tentative combination of allies may then be: oilseed producers, the oilseed control board, meat and egg producers, and the mass media. In such an alliance the following major issues will arise.

1. The major issue for the oil processors will be the market-share split.

2. The major issue for the meat and egg producers will be the animal feed prices.

3. The major issue for the oilseed control board and the oilseed farmers will be the price they receive for seeds.

4. The major issue for the mass media will be that the consumer gets a fair deal in butter and margarine pricing.

On the basis of its assessment of the alliance's probable success, the firm now estimates the extent to which its objectives should be redefined.

It might decide that in the course of time it can aim for relaxation of the *total* restrictions on margarine to allow X tons of production per annum and that it will be able to capture Y percent of the market. Since the support that the alliance obtains from the meat and egg producers is more important than the profits obtained from feeds, it could decide that a reduced feed price should be offered as an inducement for support.

In this case, the set of allies was fairly obvious. In more complex cases, this will not be so, since a complete set of critical decision areas, not just one, would be dealt with and a potential ally in one area may be incompatible in another.

The firm now starts manipulating to set up the alliance. The firm needs to approach its competitors with the idea of presenting a united front to two major groups, the oilseed control board and the meat and egg control boards. The idea would be to "threaten," in an indirect way, that seed prices must come down and that feed prices must go up. With a *united* front this threat can be made persuasively. Objections from the boards would be met with the "explanation" that the situation is not like that in other countries where all parties benefit from the large profits reaped from margarine manufacture. The delicate part of this consists of persuading competitors to go along with the "threat," ensuring that the firm gets a fair share of the end result.

Once a tentative alliance with the boards is established, the media can be appraised of the "conflict" that is taking place, where the emphasis would be (a) on the high cost of margarine compared to the cost of butter for the *consumer* media, (b) the reasons for the high cost of feeds, and (c) the reasons for the low price for seeds in the *agricultural* press.

Once this alliance has formed, the offensive and defensive strategies can be developed.

OFFENSIVE AND DEFENSIVE STRATEGIES

Offensive Strategy

Exploitation of Opposition's Weaknesses

The major weaknesses of the opposition arise from the fact that butter must be imported in times of drought and that butter is expensive and prices increase during a drought. This weakness can be exploited whenever there is a period of drought, when butter has to be imported (necessitating expenditure of foreign resources) and when all the livestock farmers (including the dairy farmers!) are obliged to buy feeds at higher prices at a time they can least afford it.

Erosion of
Opposition's Strengths

The major strength of the opposition lies in the autonomy of the dairy control board. This can be eroded by creation of pressures on several fronts for legislation to alter the legislation protecting the control board.

Defensive Strategy

Covering of Alliance's
Weaknesses

The major weakness of the alliance is the apathy of the consumers—the interest of consumer groups must be aroused by mass media publicity when butter imports start coming in or when a price increase is suggested. The high price of meat as a result of the cost of feeds can also be brought to their attention.

Preventing Erosion
of Alliance's Strengths

The strengths of the alliance are least effective in times of good rainfall, when there are no imports and prices of butter and feeds are coming down.

The essence of the *timing* of strategy emerges here. It may take many years to implement a strategy in which legislation has to be changed. There are times in this period when odds are in the favor of the opposition and times when the alliance has the upper hand.

The second essence, that of the *focus* of strategy, emerges here. Nothing can be done until legislation has been changed. The decision makers are located in the legislature, and the final focus should be on the legislature. An understanding of the process whereby legislature decisions are made is therefore necessary.

To summarize briefly, legislators are pressured by constituents to enact legislation. Powerful and influential constituents channel demands from the political "market" to legislators, who try to formulate policy to handle these demands. In so doing, they touch bases with the administrative or executive functions of the government.

In this situation what Alpha and the alliance must do is to create the pressures on the legislators and ensure strong support for these pressures from the administration.

The final strategy, therefore, is to attack whenever there are periods of drought, particularly when these are accompanied by low foreign exchange reserves and balance of payment difficulties. This attack should take place at three levels. First, the consumer public should be activated via consumer group and media action, and the agricultural public should be activated via the agricultural press. This is not particularly difficult for those media who seriously consider their role as guardians of their constituents' interests. This will give rise to pressures on legislators.

Second, the key influencers in the farm lobby should be identified. These are usually a relatively small number of opinion leaders in each farming community, and particular attention should be focused in areas where extensive egg, meat, and oilseed production takes place. Such opinion leaders may also be members of the legislature!

Third, the key administrators in the executive body should be identified. In this case treasury officials, and meat, oilseed, and egg control board officials are held responsible for the execution of legislative policy and are the targets of the public ire when the public is aroused.

The strategy would then be to wait for periods of drought and/or low reserves of foreign exchange and then "push" prices on feeds as hard as possible, to depress prices for oilseeds as low as possible, and via the media to ensure that every butter import is made dramatically visible and that every increase in butter price is made dramatically visible.

At the same time, the sales staffs of the oilseed producers should be relaying the reasons for high feed prices to the opinion leaders (who, incidentally, are often the biggest buyers) in the meat and egg farming community. Finally, the purchasing staff should be active among the opinion leaders of the oilseed farming community.

If the attack is repeated every time a drought condition occurs, the strengths of the opposition will become eroded as the dairy board and the dairy control bill supporters come under fire, in situations where they are least able to justify themselves. Eventually the Board will be forced to the point where they will be prepared to negotiate concessions.

And it is here that the final nuances of a well-conceived political strategy are played out. First, Alpha and its allies must recognize the *vast* difference between legislation that *completely prohibits* margarine production and legislation that *restricts* margarine production. In the second case, the thin edge of the wedge that will break the whole structure is in place, and it is vitally important to recognize that the initial negotiation to relax prohibition is part of a grander strategy. Probably the best they should shoot for is import replacement, subject to being allowed to produce the same amount in nondrought years. Later strategy can be devoted to improving this position.

Second, Alpha should recognize that the negotiation will create two major opportunities, one to stabilize the industry by indirect accommodation and the other to establish a high price for the margarine. For it must be recognized that the dairy board will come to the negotiating table with the express purpose of defending the interests of the dairy industry. They will, therefore, make strong demands to hold the price of margarine at levels which will not make the difference between butter and margarine too large and will demand guarantees that margarine producers will comply with quotas. Then the oilseed processors *all* can be "forced" to commit themselves to a high pricing structure and market-sharing agreement that will be legally sanctioned, all the while steadfastly arguing for a lower price and freedom of market.

This concludes the broad-brush analysis of the Alpha Oil Mills case. The purpose here was to overview the development of political strategy suggested in chapter 7.

In the next case (A. Bailey) we will focus in more detail on another set of concepts—the concepts of strategic anticipation, analysis of key decision makers, and analysis of a threat and an opportunity.

9

Illustrative Case Study:
A. Bailey (Pty), Ltd

BAILEY CASE [1]

BACKGROUND TO THE COMPANY

This equipment company has been in existence for nearly thirty years. It was started by an Englishman, Alan Bailey, a civil engineer who had been employed in his native land by a firm of consultants specializing in sewage treatment. His work brought him into contact with a firm of equipment suppliers, and, hearing that they were on the look out for a man to sell their products in Australia, he volunteered his services.

Alan Bailey was soon on his way to Sydney, where he made contact with a couple of ex-university friends who had immigrated before the war and who now had some seniority in a local firm of consulting civil engineers. Within weeks of his arrival, Alan had his first order. Being something of an opportunist, Alan wrote straight back to his principals, handing in his notice but begging to be allowed to remain a local agent for all the British company's products and enclosing a copy of the order. Much to Bailey's surprise, his terms were accepted, and he straightaway registered the company as A. Bailey (Pty), Ltd, sewage engineers.

[1] The author wishes to thank R. W. Batson for his assistance in developing this case in its original form.

In spite of Bailey's initial success, the first ten years were not easy. Money was always short, and strange things sometimes happened to his equipment. At certain times of the year the whole process would suddenly "invert," and, instead of the solid matter in the sewage settling on the tanks while the clear liquid decanted off, the reverse would happen.

Bailey gradually modified his equipment to combat this and other local problems arising from differences in diet and high ambient temperatures. He added bits of equipment from other manufacturers to his range and employed a biochemist to sort out his process problems.

By 1960, A. Bailey (Pty), Ltd, held over 60 percent of the market and was considered the expert in sewage in the country. Its customers were almost entirely in the municipalities, where the engineers tended to be extremely conservative in their outlook, preferring to deal with people and equipment that were well tried and tested.

ADVENT OF COMPETITION

Bailey's problems started when people in the Western world really began to worry about pollution. In the 1960s pollution became the "in" word and many companies (busy with their strategic planning) realized that here was an area where large sums of money would soon be spent by industrialists and municipalities forced by the sheer weight of public opinion to clear up their effluents. Millions of dollars and pounds and francs were spent by these companies in developing processes, equipment, and techniques to combat pollution, and millions more were spent trying to persuade the industrialists and local authorities to buy them—generally unsuccessfully. In order to spread their overheads more thinly, these manufacturers decided to widen their markets and "discovered" Australia.

Armed with new processes, new equipment, and marginal costing, they invaded the quiet sanctuaries of city engineers department and demanded to be heard. No one wanted to listen. After all, even though a sewage plant might work in Brussels, this didn't mean it would work in Broken Shoe.

"Sure," said the competitors, "but instead of taking you to Adelaide to see a sewage plant, we will take you to Fontainebleau and then on to Paris and Hamburg and Stockholm and London." Visibly affected by the sudden technical advantages of this new process, many engineers modified their overly conservative attitudes. On the new equipment supplied the sewage inverted in the tanks. This was a case of teething troubles, of course. Many new plants were still having sporadic teething troubles after two years of service.

At the time of the case, in 1970, A. Bailey (Pty), Ltd, has 20 percent of the market. Alan himself is old, tired, and ready to hand over to his son, Jeff.

THE SITUATION AS JEFF BAILEY SEES IT

National Trends

Australia is becoming increasingly aware of the dangers of pollution and the shortage of water. Domestic effluent is being treated and recycled in western Australia. The Ministry of Water Affairs is setting even stricter standards for effluents. Untreated sewage may not be discharged directly into the sea. Industrial effluents are being checked.

Conferences are being held in Sydney, Melbourne and Perth on how to control pollution.

Populations are growing and shifting to the towns, increasing the loads on existing sewage plants. Increasing immigration adds to this load.

Currently about 70 percent of the sewage equipment market is in large towns or cities, and the balance is in small towns and more remote districts.

Trends in the Industry

The total amount of money spent per year for the treatment of liquid effluents will increase substantially due to:

1. Increases in population and industrial activity.
2. Increases in the strictness of legislation.
3. Increased public awareness of the damages of pollution.

Where groups of towns form into metropolitan areas, there could be a tendency to combine sewage flows and to treat the effluent in one super treatment works that require less labor to run and that are more resistant to "poisoning" by sudden surges of industrial effluent.

Chemical, as opposed to biological, treatment will come into favor, either on its own, or as a tertiary stage, to bring the final effluent up to drinking-water standards.

Trace elements (dissolved inorganics that are present in very small quantities) are presently ignored but will increase in concentration as intentional or unintentional recycling occurs. In the United States, certain authorities are beginning to appreciate the dangers here and to look for ways of removing dissolved chemicals.

The competitive trends in the market are far from clear. Some of A. Bailey's foreign competitors have already run into trouble from underestimating the difficulties and costs involved in working so far from home. The future of some of the foreign companies seems to depend more on status and politics than on sound economic factors. The Australian market is small and very fragmented, and the competitors have resorted to maintaining a minimum staff of salespeople to run the offices.

Another unknown in this industry is the future influence of the consulting engineers. Most municipalities are too small to be able to afford their own experts in sewage plant selection and construction. This function is carried out mainly by consultants. A. Bailey can also put its expert staff at the service of a municipality.

The formation of a government body to help the municipalities design their plants cannot be ignored. There is a marked tendency to reduce the reliance upon direct labor in the operation of treatment plants. The controls are now being brought to one central control room overlooking the plant. Before long, one can expect to see completely automated plants.

For Australia and many other countries, water supply and sewage treatment are inextricably linked. Water is converted into effluent in every home, factory, and office. Fresh water is getting scarcer while consumption is going up. The time will be reached when most sewage will have to be reconverted to fresh water. This would seem to solve the problem.

It doesn't, however, since there are inevitable losses from evaporation, seepage, and poisoning. Planners are worried that within generations water demands may be such that supplies of fresh water will be insufficient to make up for losses—in other words, there won't be enough sewage!

Large municipalities have their own sewage experts. Their new treatment plants are worth millions of dollars each, and the international companies fight with each other to win the tenders. The large municipalities are very fussy clients to work for.

Small municipalities normally employ consultants to carry out feasibility studies, recommend processes, prepare tenders, and run the contracts.

Jeff also learned that the Ministry of Water Affairs Effluent Research Unit was taking a very active interest and that some interesting processes were under development in their laboratories.

The Current Position
for A. Bailey (Pty), Ltd

The sewage treatment market will expand in the future.   Jeff Bailey's problem is to expand his company's share of the market, to hold his increased share, and to make certain that his operations are profitable.   Although A. Bailey (Pty), Ltd, is a local company, it still imports 75 percent of its equipment from the United Kingdom, Germany, and the United States and modifies it for local conditions.

Jeff Bailey now has to decide what to do.   Obviously he will undertake a political strategy!

Figure 9.1. Analysis of the Total Situation.

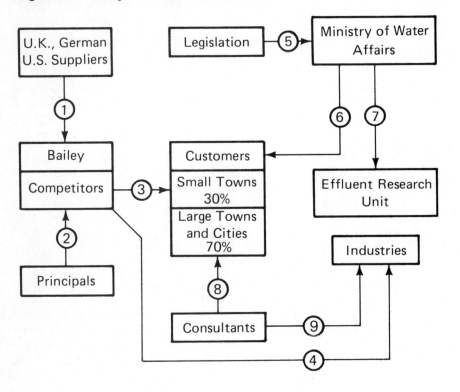

To cover a lot of detailed ground as painlessly as possible, let us summarize the main conclusions that emerged from the economic strategy analysis that Bailey made (along the lines of Hofer and Schendel) and proceed immediately to the political strategy phase.

Analysis of the Total Situation

The material parts of the system are summarized in Figure 9.1. Bailey gets equipment from overseas suppliers (1) and modifies it. Competitors' sales offices get equipment from overseas principals (2). Bailey and the competitors supply their equipment to two major markets, sewage plants to municipalities (3) and effluent plants to industry (4). At present about 70 percent of the sewage equipment market is in large towns and cities. The two markets are regulated by legislation (5) that is administered by the Ministry of Water Affairs (6), which also supports the Effluent Research Unit (7). Both municipalities (8) and industry (9) are served by consultants, who advise on the installation of new plants.

After some consideration of the trends in the environment, Jeff Bailey decided that the following were the major threat and opportunity.

Major Threat

Bailey would not be able to keep up to date on new technology being developed by the huge overseas principals of the competitors and would be by-passed.

Major Opportunity

Bailey could establish himself as a local service-oriented effluent treatment and water recovery equipment supplier.

Other alternatives, such as becoming a consultant or selling out, were considered but rejected for various reasons. (Being a consultant conflicts with being an equipment supplier, which is where his major investment is *now*. In addition there is currently an "oversupply" of consultants.) The political strategy should therefore be focused on creating conditions in the environment that will enhance the opportunity of developing as a local service-oriented company in the face of major competitors who can by-pass the company via new technology.

POLITICAL ANALYSIS:
OPPORTUNITY FOR BAILEY

In order to start formulating the political strategy, we must first analyze the total situation from a political perspective. As was mentioned in chapter 8, each of the cases will be used to highlight different aspects of the whole process of political strategy. In this case, the focus is going to be on unfolding and identifying the implications of the situation to key decision makers in each critical area.

The first analysis will be concerned with the decision-making process for sewage equipment supply in a municipality or industrial plant. There appear to be two major types of systems in municipalities.

FOR LARGE MUNICIPALITIES

For large municipalities, the process is depicted in Figure 9.2.

Figure 9.2.   Equipment Selection Decisions in Municipalities.

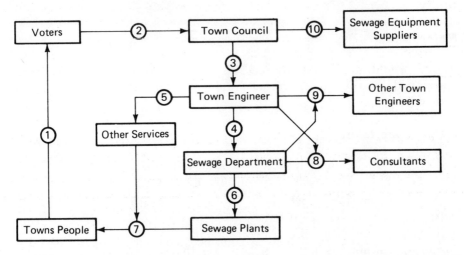

The townspeople via a voting process (1) elect a town council (2), which appoints a town engineer (3), who in turn appoints sewage experts (4) and other departments (5) to run the sewage plants (6) that provide sewage treatment and other services to the town (7). In the selection of equipment, the sewage experts and the town engineers tend to use consultants (8) or to consult other town engineers (9) to develop a specification for the plant, and then a public call for quotes is made via the town council (10), which under advisement from the town engineer selects from the tenders submitted by the equipment suppliers.

FOR SMALL MUNICIPALITIES

The main difference for small municipalities is that the town engineer does not have the funds for a sewage department expert and generally has to act as "expert" for *all* the services such as gas, electricity, water, sewage, roads, and so on. He is therefore in a much more difficult position as far as equipment selection, as well as equipment operation, is concerned. He must rely far more heavily on inputs from other town engineers or, if he can afford it, consultants.

FOR INDUSTRIAL PLANTS

Essentially, a similar equipment selection process occurs with industrial plants. In the case of industrial plants, it is usually the *works* engineer who develops the specifications and the *board* or *capital committee* that puts out the tender. Once again, large industries tend to have effluent experts in-house, while small industries tend to regard the works manager as the "resident effluent expert."

Bailey needs to recognize that there are several key factors in these decision-making systems. First, it is the town engineer or works engineer who is held *responsible* for plant operation and who thus has a major vested interest in the equipment selection decisions.

Second, sewage and effluent plants are not exactly in the mainstream of the community or industry activity, but they *are* a considerable nuisance when they are not functioning correctly. Both effluent and sewage plants are most visible to the constituents when they are *not* working. The engineer is rarely commended for how *well* they are working but is generally the focus of a lot of negative inputs when they are not.

Third, the smaller the organization, the more serious it is for the engineer, since he cannot draw on in-house expertise to get the plant in operation again.

What starts to emerge here is that the engineer, particularly of small operations, will be concerned with two factors that will be of elemental interest to him in selection of equipment—reliability, in that he does not want it to break down, and service when it does.

POLITICAL STRATEGY FORMULATION: OPPORTUNITY FOR BAILEY

Let us now go back and look at Bailey's situation in a power and influence context. What Bailey can do at this point that *none of his competitors can do* is effectively to provide specific after-sales service. He is the only person in the equipment supplier industry who has the people qualified to get a plant that is malfunctioning back to normal under *local conditions*. This constitutes a particular inducement to potential purchasers and is thus a power resource. The question is whether it is *strategic*.

To decide this, we need to look at the competitors' position. At present they are trying to keep overheads down in a highly fragmented and not particularly rich market. They are operating sales offices and do not have the field personnel to provide breakdown service in a big way. Even if they wanted to do so, they need time and resources to train people to operate the equipment under local conditions.

The fact is that Bailey's inducement resource (service) therefore constitutes an important strategic power resource, because the symbionts have limited alternatives and the commensals will take time to replicate this service—*if* they can afford to do so!

However, Bailey has the problem of convincing his symbionts that the service is worthwhile and that it will be available. The traditional approach might be to undertake an intensive industrial marketing effort. The political approach calls for a detailed political analysis with the intent of restructuring conditions so that Bailey can achieve the same purposes.

If we think about it, the basic problem is one of persuading the opponents—a problem of changing perceptions. We therefore need to consider influence processes.

Let us analyze the system developed in Figure 9.2 and ask ourselves where the dominant influence patterns are. In order to have influence, we need to establish audience, provide strategic information, and control commitments. The question we should ask ourselves is who in the system has audience with the town engineer (or works engineer in the industrial effluent case). The key influencers in the process of equipment selection appear to be other town engineers (via the grapevine) and particularly the consultants. If Bailey can induce the consultants to recommend him rather than others, he will be in a very strong position.

A consultant is ill advised to ally himself to a particular manufacturer, for fear of besmirching his reputation for objectivity (one of the reasons Bailey did not think it could operate a credible consulting service and still be an equipment supplier). However, we need to explore the dependency relation between consultant and engineer in more detail.

Let us first look at the interaction between the engineer and the consultant. The role of the consultant is to assist the engineer in writing a specification that will go out to public tender. What Bailey would want to have is a situation where the alternatives available to the town council are reduced to one—A. Bailey, Ltd. He has something to offer that no other manufacturer can offer, and that is field service. Therefore, if he can get the specifications written in such a way that after-sales service is guaranteed as a condition of tender, he will effectively lock out his competitors, who cannot meet this guarantee.

The problem then becomes one of inducing the consultants to include this guarantee. How do we do this? We return to an analysis of the dependency relation between consultant and engineer.

Let us now look at the process whereby the engineer chooses a consultant. The chances are that he will either use one he has used successfully before or that he will go through the grapevine and ask other engineers what they think. The consultants are in competition with one another, and they compete on the basis of reputation via the grapevine. Consulting engineers generally do not advertise so it is very difficult to break into the grapevine and more difficult to differentiate yourself from equally competent consultants. If a consultant can find a way of differentiating himself from his competitors in a way that enhances his reputation, he will welcome it.

Once Bailey recognizes this, it is easy to see that a consultant has a very high incentive to write a specification that contains a clause requiring certain after-sales breakdown service guarantees. In this way he becomes the *only* consultant in the industry that demands this highly beneficial clause.

For those engineers who consider such protection important, the consultants prestige will be considerably enhanced. For those engineers with in-house expertise the clause may not be all that important, but the fact that it was available would still make the consultants' role as a protector of their interests dramatically visible.

So if Bailey can get one consultant to include this clause in one contract, the grapevine will start transmitting it. Instead of a vague promise of service, a tangible guarantee is offered.

But what will happen now? Other consultants may be forced to "match the offer" to reduce the gap between the service they offer and that of the first. If they do this, where does that leave the first consultant?

Here lies the key for Bailey's negotiation with that first consultant. If other consultants *are* eventually going to follow suit, then the only differentiation that the first consultant can achieve is being the *first* one in the industry to introduce the clause. And the more "successful" the clause is, the more important it is to be the first. Therefore, in the negotiation with the consultant he selects, Bailey has a powerful bargaining base. In effect, he is giving the consultant an opportunity that can easily be given to someone else.

It therefore appears that the environment can be restructured to suit Bailey's purpose by an influence play, after which he will emerge as the only alternative available to those engineers in the market who want guaranteed after-sales breakdown service.

The tentative alliance that he needs to create as far as his opportunity is concerned is with a number of consultants whose only contribution will be to include a breakdown service guarantee in the tender specification. His first move should be to see just one consultant who is prepared to do this.

STRATEGIC ANTICIPATION: OPPORTUNITY FOR BAILEY

How will the competitors respond?

First, we have seen that competitors have succeeded in taking away many engineers by taking them to "inspect" overseas plants. This is a major weakness that Bailey has not matched, and the chances are that competitors will increase these types of efforts in response to the guarantee clause.

Second, we can expect them to start moving toward a more service-oriented business. Perhaps some will consider importing and training a field force. Probably they will consider luring away Bailey's own people to join them and provide this service.

Let us now look at the problem of establishing service-oriented businesses from the perspective of the decision makers in the competitors' organizations. It appears that they are under pressure to keep overheads down. Any additions to personnel, particularly ones in which there is a long lag between incurring the expense and getting benefits from the expense, will make their position here difficult with the overseas headquarters. It is therefore more likely that, if they match Bailey at all, they will try to do it by drawing away Bailey's personnel. Bailey must ensure that his field experts are given very little incentive to move.

Also, Bailey's competitors appear to be more interested in the large plants. Small, remote plants are probably regarded as a necessary evil. It seems likely that they will gladly forgo that part of the market initially.

Finally, this is a situation of many symbionts and few commensals, and it is going to be very expensive for each competitor in the industry as a whole to develop and maintain a field sales force.

The interesting possibility that emerges from the analysis is that Bailey can undertake breakdown service (and commissioning, perhaps) on behalf of the entire industry by structuring a subsidiary that will subcontract breakdown work for all installations that desire it.

Once Bailey has recovered sufficient share of the market to have the impact of his strategy sufficiently severe that the competitors will start considering a counter move, he can stabilize that share by approaching them with the very rational offer of creating a (very lucrative for him) field breakdown service subsidiary. The theme of his negotiating strategy here will be that he will be saving each member of the industry the cost of taking on, training, and maintaining their own field service teams. Remember that they are currently under pressure to keep costs down in the highly fragmented and rather unprofitable market they face. In exchange for doing so he may convince them to stay out of the small plant market and leave it to him.

Let us return now to the other response he can expect, that of increased overseas trips for potential buyers. What Bailey needs to recognize is that he too has overseas principals whose large equipment he imports and who would like to see him regain his share of the market. *If* he elects to match his competitors' rather dubious sales methods, there is no reason that the principals should not share in the costs of such methods. The theme emerges again: why try to do something on our own if we can find allies who are able to assist us?

POLITICAL STRATEGY: OPPORTUNITY FOR BAILEY

For the opportunity for Bailey, we see the following offensive and defensive strategies emerging.

OFFENSIVE STRATEGY

Exploit Opponents' Weaknesses

Form an alliance with one or more consultants to have a guaranteed breakdown service clause included in the tender specification. This should firmly secure a large part of the small-plant market and some of the large-plant market.

Erode Opponents' Strengths

Match opponents' overseas junket offer with offers supported in large part by Bailey's overseas suppliers, *provided* this is not against Bailey's principles.

DEFENSIVE STRATEGY

Block Erosion of Bailey's Own Strengths

When competitors start showing signs of matching Bailey with their own field force (*someone* in A. Bailey, Ltd., will be approached to join such a force), propose that Bailey form a subsidiary that will provide industry-wide breakdown maintenance.

Prevent Exploitation of Own Weaknesses

In this case the same as eroding opponents' strengths.

POLITICAL ANALYSIS:
MAJOR THREAT TO BAILEY

The major threat Bailey sees is that, due to the lack of resources, the company cannot invest the funds to keep abreast of technology he runs the risk of being "leap frogged" and left behind in technology. The political approach argues that, if he hasn't the resources to do something, he should try to find someone who will do it for him.

In Bailey's case, the organizations to do it for him are obvious—his overseas suppliers and the Effluent Research Unit of the Ministry of Water Affairs.

Starting with the Effluent Research Unit, we are going to focus in this case on the decision-making systems of our opponents. Let us look at the system in some detail.

Bailey needs to ask himself what type of person works in such a department, where the pay is often less than elsewhere in the country. There appear to be three types: 1. people who out of a sense of dedication to the patriotic need for Australia to handle its water problems want to help; 2. people who out of dedication to science want to do research; 3. people who enjoy the security of a government job.

If the key decision makers in the Effluent Research Unit are of the first or second type, then Bailey has a high chance of establishing audience with them, because he is a "lone Australian doing battle with large overseas interests"—which could appeal to the patriots—and he is the acknowledged Australian expert and has a wealth of practical knowledge regarding the design, development, and operation of sewage and effluent plants under Australian conditions—which could appeal to the scientists.

Ideally, what Bailey needs to do is establish an alliance with members of the Effluent Research Unit whereby he can keep up to date in technology. He needs to consider what he can bring to such an alliance. A review of what he can bring is the following:

1. If he takes the trouble to secure it, information from his German, British, and American principals on the "state of the art" in the technology of these countries and materials on the latest developments in their research efforts.

2. Equipment, field personnel, and occasionally funds that will be useful for the researchers in supplementing the funds they need to carry out research projects.

3. Knowledge regarding the applications and operation of actual plants, knowledge of plant conditions and operational changes required under different conditions in Australia.

4. Actual plants out in the field on which pilot research or full-scale research can be carried out, together with a field force who can get it working again when things go wrong!

So, from the point of view of the Effluent Research Unit scientists, there are substantial benefits in working *with* Bailey in bringing new technology to fruition under Australian conditions. They can work on the basic research, and he can help them convert from basic research to applications.

STRATEGIC ANTICIPATION: THREAT TO BAILEY

How would the competitors respond to a move by Bailey to start working with the Effluent Research Unit?

The question is whether they will do anything at all! At present they do not have the expertise to match what Bailey can bring to the Unit, and at this point they are under severe profit pressure, so there are not many funds. They are unlikely to be able to understand the results of the research or to carry out the conversions. And, finally, they are not Australian.

As time goes by these conditions are likely to change. More sophisticated operations are likely to be set up by the competitors as the market expands to justify them. If Bailey is to take advantage of his position, it must be in the few years before these more sophisticated operations are installed. If any of the competitors does try to move closer, Bailey can, by performance, take every opportunity to demonstrate time and again the vast difference between what he can bring to the Effluent Research Unit and what they can bring.

Over the next few years, an intensely reciprocative and personal relationship between Bailey and the Effluent Research Unit can be developed. Then when the competitors try to move in Bailey will have developed a great deal of authority in the eyes of the Unit, and it will take a long time for that authority to be eroded.

POLITICAL STRATEGY:
MAJOR THREAT TO BAILEY
OFFENSIVE STRATEGY

Exploit Opponents' Weaknesses

Use the fact that Bailey is Australian and experienced in Australian operations to secure audience. Emphasize that at this stage the competition cannot meet these requirements.

Erode Opponents' Strengths

Develop a position of authority with the Effluent Research Unit and a working relationship whereby Bailey and the Unit undertake joint projects in converting new Australian technology to operating plants.

DEFENSIVE STRATEGY

Prevent Erosion
of Our Strengths

Demonstrate, via performance, the vast difference between Bailey and competitors in capability to convert from laboratory to full-scale operation.

Prevent Exploitation
of Our Weaknesses

Input latest technology via overseas principals to the Effluent Research Unit.

This concludes the political strategy for this case. Once again, it must be emphasized that the cases are illustrative rather than comprehensive. For this reason the discussion was restricted to one opportunity and one threat. In the real-life situation, more opportunities and threats would be identified and explored by similar processes. Options unexplored, for instance, include the possibility of merging with a larger competitor. Even in this case, Bailey should go to the merger from a position of strength, with regained market share and a robust competitive position.

SUMMARY

In this case the prime focus was on looking at the nature of the decision making that takes place in the critical elements' systems. We saw that, through exploration of the dependencies between these elements and their systems, the possibilities for indirect political action became evident. [In the previous case (that of Alpha Oil Mills), more attention was given to relations between systems, and we focused on the process of carrying out a political strategy formulation.]

In the next case, more attention will be given to *analysis of alternative structures* and *formulation of negotiating strategies.*

10

Illustrative Case Study: Apollo Wholesalers

APOLLO WHOLESALER'S PROBLEM

Jack Walliser, managing director of Apollo Wholesalers, a household products wholesaler, was busy with a problem facing him in the sales of a household chemical called Ickygunk.

Table 10.1. Five Local Producers of Ickygunk and Their Market Shares.

Producer	Competitive Status	Ickygunk's Status in Company's Product Line	Approximate Retail Market Share. of Ickygunk Sales
Aleph	International	One of many product lines	40%
Beth	International	One of many product lines	30%
Gimel	National	One of limited product lines	15%
Daleth	Local	Sole (marginal) product	10%
Vau	Local	Sole (marginal) product	5%

Ickygunk is extremely sensitive to transport costs and can therefore be produced only locally. Walliser is certain that he is facing a cartel arrangement between the five local producers, whose share of the local market is shown in Table 10.1.

Aleph is an international company which markets a very large number of products, whereas Vau is a small regional company which only produces Ickygunk. Apollo Wholesalers is one of four major local wholesaling (Table 10.2) companies that supply a number of retail outlets in the region.

Table 10.2. Four Local Wholesalers and Their Market Shares.

Wholesaler	Approximate Retail Market Share of Ickygunk Sales
Apollo	25%
Castor	20%
Pollux	10%
Achilles	10%

The balance of Ickygunk sales is made directly from producer to three major retail chains, whose market shares are shown in Table 10.3.

Table 10.3. Three Retail Chains and Their Market Shares.

Chain Stores	Approximate Retail Market Share for Ickygunk
Wodan	15%
Thor	15%
Freia	5%

No retailer other than the chain stores has more than 1% of the market. Ickygunk is unbranded. It is basically packed into wooden boxes after being wrapped in plastic and then is sold direct from these boxes to the public. Walliser is wondering what he should do about the suspected cartel who appear to have a price agreement going: What has been happening is that all wholesalers buy Ickygunk from all the producers. Walliser has been trying every means at his disposal to get a price reduction from the producers, but no matter which supplier he approaches, he gets the same price. The other wholesalers appear to be getting the same treatment.

Walliser knows that in recent years the market for Ickygunk has been eroded by the introduction of a more sophisticated product called Yuckigunk and this has caused some overcapacity in the industry. He would therefore expect the two local producers, who are battling for profits, to be keen to come to some kind of price reduction agreement just to increase volume.

The reason Walliser wants to effect a reduction in the price of Ickygunk is twofold.

1. Retailers are complaining that the chain stores are selling Icky-gunk at prices that can only mean that the chain stores are getting a big price break from the producers and are asking for a price break for themselves.

2. Walliser has noticed with some concern the steady growth that the chain stores are achieving in the retail market. The retailers are starting to talk about forming buyers' cooperatives to develop more clout by buying in large quantities directly from the producers. Walliser feels that the days of the wholesaler dominating the household products market are numbered but also recognizes that once the shakeout is over there will always be a role to be played by the surviving wholesalers. Walliser is determined to be one of the surviving wholesalers.

To do this he has to take market share away from the competitors. He must demonstrate to the retailers that he has the ability to deliver superior performance, and Ickygunk, which constitutes about 5 percent of his current sales volume (which is quite large for a wholesaler) appears that it might be a useful test case.

The decision he must make is whether to go up against the cartel of suppliers and, if so, how to go about it.

ANALYSIS OF THE TOTAL SITUATION

The total situation is analyzed in Figure 10.1.

The system here depicts the flow of Ickygunk from production to retailer. In addition to Ickygunk, which constitutes 5 percent of Apollo's sales, the wholesaler handles a large number of other lines of household products. Many of these are supplied to Apollo through Aleph, Beth, and Gimel, who have multiple lines of products, including the competing product Yuckigunk, which now constitutes a good 3 percent of sales but appears to be leveling off.

Figure 10.1. Analysis of the Ickygunk System.

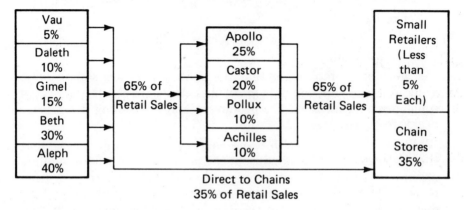

Walliser must take care not to antagonize the producers, who currently supply him with about 40 percent of his total sales. In addition, he has other suppliers who supply the remaining 60 percent of his total sales.

Finally, for each of the product lines that Apollo handles, Walliser's sales are in the region of 25 percent of the retail market, as with Ickygunk.

The above discussion is summarized in Figure 10.2.

Figure 10.2. Apollo Wholesalers' Overall Sales Structure.

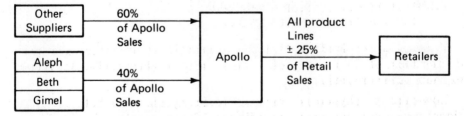

The critical elements in the system are obviously the chain stores and producers, who are potential opponents in a price cut play, and other wholesalers and retailers who would benefit from a price cut and are thus potential allies.

However, since Walliser is intent on cutting into the other whole-salers' market share this disqualifies them as allies. He also feels that the small retailers are individually too weak and collectively too dispersed and disorganized to be of much use.

The attempt at political strategy should therefore be viewed as something he will have to do on his own. The first step is an analysis of the opponents, in which Walliser attempts to determine the system flows of his opponents.

ANALYSIS OF OPPONENTS

Analysis of the opponents reveals that there are three major types of opponents.

INTERNATIONAL PRODUCERS

The system for international producers appears in Figure 10.3.

Figure 10.3. International Producers: Ickygunk System.

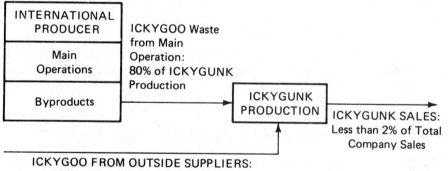

What Walliser finds is that the international producers are pro-ducing most of their Ickygunk from a waste product (called Ickygoo) of their other operations.

Low-quality Ickygoo is converted to Ickygunk. For both interna-tional producers, however, insufficient Ickygoo waste is available, so low-quality Ickygoo is purchased from outside suppliers, and about 20 percent of final sales is purchased for this purpose.

He also finds that Ickygunk is about 2 percent or less of each com-pany's total sales.

NATIONAL PRODUCER (GIMEL)

The system for the national producer is similar. Gimel also produces Ickygunk from low-quality waste Ickygoo, but in this case about 15 percent of total sales are made from poor-quality Ickygoo purchased from outside suppliers. Ickygunk sales are about 2 percent of Gimel's total sales.

REGIONAL PRODUCER

Finally Daleth and Vau, whose sale product is Ickygunk, produced all their sales from Ickygoo that is purchased from outside suppliers.

Finally, Walliser is aware that the pattern of replacement of Ickygunk by the new product Yuckigunk is not too dissimilar from his own experience with the sales of these products. Over the years, his proportion of sales of Ickygunk have fallen from about 8 percent to a level of about 5 percent.

What does the information really mean?

Walliser knows that there is overcapacity in the industry. If sales have fallen from 8 to 5 percent, he can estimate that industry-wide capacity must be in the region of five-eighths or about 60 percent of the capacity they used to supply.

He also knows that sitting with excess capacity is expensive and that there is a high incentive to reduce overhead cost per unit sales by increasing volume. This is usually done by cutting prices, but, if there is overcapacity in the *industry*, all that results from a price cut is a price war, which can be avoided by a price cartel (which he appears to be facing).

However, if there is overcapacity in the industry he knows that there exists a great incentive for someone to cheat. In particular, if someone can find a way of cheating without being punished, he will have even more incentive to cheat.

In looking at his array of opponents, Walliser has to decide who would have the highest incentive to cheat.

The obvious ones are Daleth and Vau, the two regional purchasers whose sole product is Ickygunk and who are at present running marginal operations.

Now Walliser can do some calculating.

Currently Apollo is selling 25 percent of the market. Combined Daleth and Vau are supplying 15 percent of the market. If they had held market share as the market declined, they should have capacity to supply ⅝ × 15 or about 24 percent of the market. The main thing that would be stopping them from cutting prices to gain market share would be the punitive retaliation from the other, larger producers.

However, let us look now at the decision-making systems of the other producers. Ickygunk sales constitute a very small proportion of the total sales of the companies. This causes us to raise some questions:

1. What is the reason for a cartel in the first place?
2. What kind of decision maker is going to be making the decisions regarding Ickygunk prices?

If we take a good look at the system shown in Figure 10.3, we can perhaps see the answer to question 1. Ickygunk is a profitable way of getting rid of what would otherwise be a major nuisance—Icky-goo waste. The last thing that any of the big producers would want to get stuck with is a waste product piling up at the end of their production systems. The only reason they would want to come to some kind of stabilizing cartel arrangement would be to stop the smaller producers from taking away market share until the big producers *do* have Ickygoo piling up in their warehouses. Once a stabilized situation has been reached, at a profitable price, why not buy some low-quality Ickygoo and turn more of a profit making more Ickygunk?

But the purpose of risking a cartel agreement is to stop waste Ickygoo from piling up, *not* to hold prices. If this is the case, some more figuring can be done. At present about 20 percent of Aleph's and Beth's sales and 10 percent of Gimel's sales of Ickygunk are made from outside supplies. With Aleph and Beth having 70 percent of the current market and Gimel having 15 percent, this means that $(0.20 \times 70) + (0.1 \times 15)$ or about 15 percent of their current sales are made from *outside supplies*.

Let's put the figuring all together. Apollo sells 25 percent of the retail market. Daleth and Vau sell 15 percent together but possibly could produce another 8 percent making about 23 percent of the retail market. And Aleph, Beth, and Gimel can lose a total of 15 percent of the market before they start getting really violent about price cuts.

It appears that it may be possible to persuade Daleth and Vau to join in an alliance with Apollo to cut their prices in exchange for a *guaranteed* increase in volume to about 60 percent more than they are currently producing yet still not reach a market-share level that will get the opposition to a point where they are not able to use up their current waste. The question is how likely are the big producers to accept this arrangement without taking punitive action?

STRATEGIC ANTICIPATION

How will the big producers respond? To answer this, we need to answer the question 2 asked above: what kind of decision maker is going to make the Ickygunk price decision?

The question Walliser had to ask himself was "If I were in charge of a large international company operating in this country, who would I put in charge of a waste product operation that sells less than 2 percent of my total sales?" You can bet the answer would not be a hard-minded, aggressive, and sharp manager destined for the top. Walliser could guess that the person in charge of Ickygunk activities would almost certainly be someone who would not be prepared to rock the boat. He would be more concerned with not piling up waste in front of production processes making main-line products, because he would be assessed more on disruption of production than on departmental profits.

What it boils down to is that if we get into the decision-making level of the opponent, we recognize that we are not taking on the mighty Aleph or Beth or Gimel as *organizations* but are taking on a *person* and in this case a person who probably has very little political capability. The main thing we must do is keep from causing that person to panic. He needs to be persuaded that he is not going to face a problem of excess Ickygoo.

So, if Walliser plays his cards right and negotiates well, he can anticipate that Aleph, Beth, and Gimel will hold prices and reduce production by reducing outside purchases. The next problem to be addressed is the one of developing a negotiating strategy.

NEGOTIATING STRATEGY

For all the opponents, the main issue appears to be one of *price* at this stage. What Walliser must do is break the coalitions by focusing attention on the *volume* issue. These were the two major issues. He knew that he had sufficient sales to be able to handle all the volume, up to Vau and Daleth's *original* capacity, if they decided to give him a price break. He also wanted to *lock his competitors out* of any price reduction if possible, because he was intent on a grander strategy of demonstrating to retailers that Apollo was the wholesaler they should support. This introduced a third issue, exclusivity of price reductions. Walliser accordingly set down the issues and their priorities for each party (Table 10.4).

Table 10.4.   Issue Priorities in Negotiation.

Issue	Walliser	Small Producers	Big Producers
Price	2	2	1
Volume	3	1	2 conditional
Exclusivity	1	3	3

When we consider the issues in terms of priorities we see three distinct patterns emerge. For Walliser, if he cannot get some exclusivity he may as well not get price reductions, so exclusivity is his first priority. He knows he can handle the volume, so volume is his lowest priority.

For the small producers, the issue of volume is probably the most urgent. If they can raise their volumes, they can increase profits and to some extent can reduce prices. The least of their worries is Walliser's concern with exclusivity.

For the big producers, the issue of price is paramount, because they can adjust volume via outside purchases. However, *if volume falls below a certain level, price becomes unimportant.* They too could care less about Walliser's concern with exclusivity.

It is obvious from looking at these issues that two separate negotiating strategies are required, one for small and one for big producers.

The sequence appears to be that Walliser should negotiate with the small producers to ascertain their interest in increasing volume and then with the large producers to allay their fears that they will end up in a position of oversupply. This he can do only when he has some assurance that he will have the support of the smaller producers.

In formulating his negotiating strategy for the smaller producers, the order for negotiation appears to be volume, price, and exclusivity for the following reasons: Walliser can start the negotiations by implying that he is considering increasing his orders to take up to 150 percent of their current total orders, and he wants to know whether this is possible.

Once the small producers have got thoroughly interested about this, he can start talking price. The key bluff Walliser can use is that if he does not get what he wants from the small producer he can go to the others. He will then reveal that he has sufficient evidence of a price agreement to make things rather uncomfortable if the suppliers act uncooperatively. He will also reveal that he is prepared to arrange with the other producers for them not to take punitive action.

When the small producer still shows reluctance to take a price cut, he can suggest that he take an option to buy all their production for the next two years, provided this does not exceed 150 percent of their current total sales. The option will have a time limit, and, if he exercises the option, he will agree to a contract in which a price, to be agreed later, is set. In this way he can guarantee his exclusivity without even having it enter the agenda as a bargaining point. (Notice the difference if he starts the negotiation with the issue of exclusivity. This provides the *producer* with a lever.)

Once he has the options, he can now go to the large producers. In the case of the large producers the agenda would be price, volume, and exclusivity, in that order.

Here Walliser can start negotiations by emphasizing that he has no intention of changing the price structure of the large producers but that he intends taking far more volume from the small producers and that this will probably reduce the market-share large producers will be selling. He will hasten to add that this will in no way reduce their volume to the extent that they will be sitting with excess *stock*. In fact, Apollo will be prepared to take off any excess stock at current prices, if they want him to do so. To demonstrate his commitment he will show them the options he has taken out with the small producers, thus also avoiding the threat they could make to the small producers since (they are committed to the transgressive act via their options). Faced with this situation, the large producers have no incentive to cut prices. Walliser obviously would prefer that they did not; hence his offer to continue to buy from them a reduced volume at their existing prices. Once again, if Walliser succeeds, he has maintained exclusivity without the issue entering the agenda.

With this strategy in mind, Walliser can now approach the small producers with the intention of negotiating a reduced price. (Or can he? The political approach suggests that, having identified critical allies or opponents, he may find it worthwhile to investigate *their* dependencies to probe for possible areas of indirect action. This has not been done.)

STRATEGY IMPLEMENTATION

In the actual case, Walliser took his negotiating strategy to the small producers and found two bitter men. A formerly lucrative business had been slowly eroded away by declining markets for Ikygunk; they were both sitting with about 55 percent of their capacity unused but still were carrying the overhead costs of the equipment and maintenance. They were desperate to increase volume, but felt that any price cut would launch a major price war that they could not survive.

Both expressed great interest in Walliser's proposal, but then the bombshell exploded. Not only were they strapped on the output side, but they were strapped on the input side. Walliser had failed to explore *their* dependencies, and both producers depended on outside suppliers for Ikygoo to make their product.

The Ickygoo system is depicted in Figure 10.4.

Figure 10.4.   System for Ickygoo.

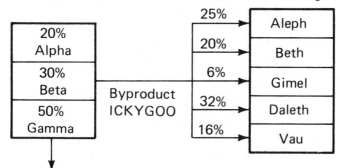

He found that Daleth and Vau depended for their supplies of Ikygoo on three major suppliers, Alpha, Beta, and Gamma, who produced low-quality Ikygoo as a by-product from the production of Goockystuff. Moreover, Alpha, Beta, and Gamma together purchased more than half of the production of this waste Ikygoo, and the suppliers were in the difficult position that they *had* to sell it or also have *their* production systems held up by excess inventories of waste product.

By acting in concert, Aleph, Beth, and Gimel had been able to take control of the raw material supply system. They were, to some extent, independent of the suppliers because they produced most of their raw material in house. By selectively "punishing" recalcitrant suppliers (merely canceling orders and letting the waste inventory pile up), they were eventually able to control how much Ickygoo would be sold to each producer and thus controlled the Ickygoo market. So, even if Daleth or Vau wanted to increase volume, they might not get the raw materials for it!

Now what was interesting was that Goockystuff was also a household chemical. (It is not unusual to have a whole network of chemicals and by-products related to one another in a "family" of chemicals, such as household chemicals.) Apollo wholesalers, as a household chemicals wholesaler, handled their lines—to the tune of 25 percent of total retail sales, as with his other lines.

With this additional information, a new dimension is added. Walliser can break the control of Aleph, Beth, and Gimel by guaranteeing to Alpha, Beta, and Gamma that he will buy up all their production of Ickygoo waste.

Alpha, Beta, and Gamma currently supply Ickygoo as shown in Table 10.5.

Table 10.5.   Percentage of Ickygoo Supplied by Alpha, Beta, and Gamma.

Company Supplied	Percentage of Ickygoo Bought Outside	Total Ickygunk Sales
Aleph	20 percent of 40 percent	8
Beth	20 percent of 30 percent	6
Gimel	15 percent of 15 percent	2
Daleth	100 percent of 10 percent	10
Vau	100 percent of 5 percent	5
Total		± 31 percent of the total Ickygunk retail sales

Moreover, Apollo has a lot of clout with Alpha Beta and Gamma because he is currently buying 25 percent of their output.

Walliser needs to recognize that here is an opportunity for Apollo to get total control of the situation by taking an option to buy all of Alpha, Beta, and Gamma's Ickygoo production.

He can thus guarantee the *suppliers* that their waste Ickygoo will be purchased and can guarantee *Daleth* and *Vau* that they will have sufficient supplies of Ickygoo to produce all the Ickygunk they want and guarantee to buy it from them (at his prices). He can then control the amount of outside Ickygoo that Aleph, Beth, and Gimel can get to make extra product. And he has the sales capacity to sell at least 25 percent of the market.

With the option to buy all the outside Ickygoo, he has provided the Aleph, Beth, and Gimel's managers a plausible reason to give *their* bosses for the decrease in sales volume—there is a shortgage of outside Ickygoo to make the product! Finally, there is no incentive for *them* to reduce prices to Apollo's competitors, so Apollo can obtain the exclusivity it is seeking if it can ensure that the large producers do not cut prices. So his negotiating strategy is now enhanced by the fact that he can ally himself with the suppliers first, to secure an option to buy all their output, then go to the small producers with an offer they can't refuse and secure options for their production, and then go to the large producers with all these options and get them to recognize that he holds the cards but will not threaten their waste disposal problem.

(As a matter of record, Walliser managed to effect a substantial price decrease and increased his market share in Ikygunk to 30 percent within a year. Five years later, by applying political strategies to his other lines, he ended up with 60 percent of the regional wholesale market.)

SUMMARY

In this case we focused on two aspects of strategy that received less emphasis in the other cases—detailed analysis of the *dependency structures* and *alternative structures* of the players, and *negotiating strategy,* a simple three-issue, two-step negotiating process in this case.

In an actual political strategy situation, it is rarely necessary to apply in detail all the concepts discussed in this book, but at different times and in different situations each of the concepts has proved useful in the formulation of a political strategy.

So the procedure outlined in chapter 7 need not be copied slavishly but rather should be used as a guideline for checking whether all the facets that *should* be considered *have* been considered.

11

Concluding Remarks

SUMMARY

This book has attempted to cover an aspect of strategy formulation that is generally ignored but often practiced—that of restructuring the environment to ensure that our economic strategy can be achieved.

The whole idea revolves around manipulation and accommodation to allies who are able to help us achieve our purposes.

We first explained the concept of manipulation and the bases of power and influence that provided guidelines for *developing* power and influence. Then we gave our attention to the concept of bargaining or negotiation and focused primarily on distributive bargaining tactics. Finally, we saw how these tactics might be put together into a negotiating strategy.

From there we turned to coalition building and internal politics of the organization. A model was developed to show how the process of policy formulation and execution takes place, and the relevance of knowledge of this process for strategy formulation was discussed.

In chapter 6 we focused on interorganizational politics first and developed the guidelines for the major thrust of a political strategy under various combinations of environmental conditions. Then we focused on strategic anticipation, that is, trying to determine what competitors' responses will occur under the given strategy. We saw

158

that the use of three models could be useful for strategic anticipation: the rational actor, the organizational process, and the bureaucratic political models.

In chapter 7 we attempted to integrate these concepts into a formal outline for developing a political strategy. This outline was then illustrated by the Alpha Oil Mills case in chapter 8.

Then specific facets of political strategy were illustrated in two more cases. In the Bailey illustration, in chapter 9, we focused on analysis of the decision-making system of the opponents. In the Apollo Wholesalers case, in chapter 10, we focused on detailed analyses of the alternative structures between opponents.

FINAL COMMENTS

It is now appropriate to make some final comments. First, a political approach to strategy formulation captures the essence of what is largely ignored yet appears to be an overriding concern of many senior managers observed in practice. The political approach provides a framework for organizing one's thoughts in addressing oneself to the aggressive, competitive strategic action that characterizes many dynamic businesspeople today. It lays the theoretical groundwork for explaining the action that aggressive managers intuitively develop in the pursuit of their corporate goals.

Second, this introductory text merely *exposes* the subject of organizational politics. There is a great deal to be explored and explained. Much work in the field is already being carried out but largely by social scientists and for organizations other than businesses. The thoughts and insights these workers are providing should be transferred to the field of management, and particularly policy, as soon as possible. Much more research needs to be done directly in the field of organizational politics in order to give more substance to the strategic decision-making process.

Third, the approach raises a need for case studies and organizational analyses that focus on the practical application of the concepts in this book to strategic situations, both in practice and for teaching purposes.

Fourth, and by no means least important, the subject matter treated in this book raises questions relating to ethics. What needs to be explored and thought through by the reader is what the limits to ethical behavior are in applying the concepts herein. It was argued that the principles in this book could be applied within the ethical constraints of the individual reader, but what are these constraints, and when do we compromise them?

REFERENCES

Allison, G. T. *Essence of Decision: Explaining the Cuban Missile Crisis.* Boston: Little Brown, 1971.

Blau, P. "Differentiation of Power" in *Political Power* by R. Bell, D. V. Edwards, and R. H. Wagner. New York: The Free Press, 1969.

Bower, J. H. *Managing the Resource Allocation Process.* Cambridge: Harvard University Press, 1970.

Chamberlain, N. W. *A General Theory of Economic Process.* New York: Harper and Brothers, 1955.

Crozier, M. *The Bureaucratic Phenomenon.* Chicago: Chicago University Press, 1971.

Cyert, R. M. and March, J. G. *A Behavioral Theory of the Firm.* Englewood Cliffs: Prentice Hall, 1964.

Emerson, R. M. "Power-dependence relations." *American Sociological Review*, 27 (February, 1962).

Karass, C. L. *The Negotiating Game.* New York: World Publishing, 1970.

Katz, D. and Kahn, R. L. *The Social Psychology of Organizations.* New York: Wiley, 1966.

Kennedy, J. "Practice and Theory in Negotiations: A Conceptual Model for Negotiations." In Webster, R. E.: *New Directions in Marketing.* Proceedings of the 48th National Conference of the American Marketing Association. Chicago: American Marketing Association, 1965.

Lederer, W. J. and Burdick, E. *The Ugly American.* New York: W. W. Norton & Co., 1958.

MacMillan, I. C. *An Analysis of Certain Power and Influence Relations between the Firm and its Environment.* Unpublished MBL dissertation, University of South Africa, 1972.

MacMillan, I. C. "Business Strategies for Political Action." *Journal of General Management*, Vol. 2, No. 1 (1974).

Marchal, J. "The Construction of a New Theory of Profit." *American Economic Review*, Vol. 41, No. 4 (1951).

March, J. G., and Simon, H. A. *Organizations.* New York: John Wiley & Sons, 1967.

Maslow, A. H. *Motivation and Personality.* New York: Harper and Row, 1954.

McGregor, D. *The Human Side of Enterprise.* New York: McGraw-Hill, 1960.

Parsons, T. C. *Politics and Social Structure.* New York: The Free Press, 1969.

Pettigrew, A. M. *The Politics of Organisational Decision-Making.* London: Tavistock, 1973.

Riker, W. H. *The Theory of Political Coalitions.* New Haven: Yale University Press, 1962.

Schein, E. H. *Organizational Psychology.* Englewood Cliffs: Prentice Hall, 1963.

Schelling, T. C. *The Strategy of Conflict.* Cambridge: Harvard University Press, 1963.

Schumpeter, J. A. *Capitalism, Socialism and Democracy.* New York: Harper Brothers, 1942.

Thompson, J. D. *Organizations in Action.* New York: McGraw-Hill, 1967.

Walton, R. E. and R. B. McKersie. *A Behavioral Theory of Labor Negotiations.* New York: McGraw-Hill, 1965.

*

Index

END OF VOLUME